DO YOU REALLY KNOW ME?

Mental Illness Nightmare Delusions

DARREN FRY

authorHOUSE®

AuthorHouse™ UK
1663 Liberty Drive
Bloomington, IN 47403 USA
www.authorhouse.co.uk
Phone: 0800 047 8203 (Domestic TFN)
     +44 1908 723714 (International)

Published by AuthorHouse 07/01/2019

ISBN: 978-1-7283-8089-6 (sc)
ISBN: 978-1-7283-8839-7 (e)

It all began when a baby was born on Tuesday 20th March 1973. Anne Kathleen Fry, my mother, went into labour on that marvellous day. Kingston surrey hospital was that place where I was born into the world. There was a complication on birth when my mother was given an epidural and then I arrived very fast. I was handed to the nurse very fast because I was slightly starved of oxygen and an oxygen mark was place on my head, it was known at the time I was slightly blue, when I was born. After I was checked I was handed into my mother's arms to begin my journey into life.

My first memories of being an infant were going to preschool/nursery in Worcester Park, Surrey. I lived in Worcester Park which was not far from my nursery/preschool with my Sister Samantha, who was born in June 1970, I was the younger sibling which isn't easy.

I grew up in a beautiful detached house with my mum, dad and sister. My dad worked hard as a self-employed greengrocer & grocer. He had a mobile shop which he sold almost everything to make ends meet to support his family. I always remember him telling me to sell jeans to ladies and Christmas trees he used to put on top of his van. My mother worked part time in universal office supplies in Merton, to pay for luxuries, such as holidays & Christmas presents, all the lovely things we all love.

I remember having a fantastic childhood. My parents took me everywhere from castles to parks and my memories of my father always coming home as I finished school to playing with me and my sister and giving us quality time, we deserved as children. My mother was always there for us because she worked while we were at school between the hours of 9am to 1pm. We went on the most fantastic holidays abroad, memories of Greece, France, and Malta to name a few.

I then progressed to go to first School which was also based in Worcester Park. I had some wonderful teachers they always thought I was a great character, funny cheeky young lad.

My time at first school was amazing, I remember learning the maypole dancing, which you don't see in schools these days. We were very lucky to have a swimming pool at our school, which sadly is no longer there. In my day there was a three-tier schooling method.

Then I moved up to Middle School also in Worcester Park, where I enjoyed another great school. Having great memories of filming at our school, which was a John Osbourne film called 'a better class of person', which was made into a film from a bestselling book. We had to have our hair cut short back and sides, which was a lot of fun for us all.

I believe I was only in one scene, coming down the stairs, but was very lucky to experience the film world at a very young age of 10 years old. They put tape on all the windows, brought in air raid shelters, all very exciting for a young lad growing up. The free cans of coke we got were the high light when we were young little things, little minds and all that. I was not awfully academic at school, but I gave it my best shot. Spellings were my best speciality, sports were not, but I did enjoy the cross country runs, well my dad picking me up in the car half way round and dropping me off to the finish line was a fond memory, anything to save energy.

We enjoyed great trips away with the school, France, the Alps has some amazing experiences.

I was always a happy young chap at school things were good. I was always close to family, love to go over to the sweet Shop, to get our jaw breaker sweets that used to last days and days and a good old slush puppy, when school was out. Oh, and not forgetting the wonderful 1p sweets and the air-conditioned shop which was absolutely fantastic.

I got into my fair share of trouble at school, which mostly started outside the classroom being the class clown. One memory was in class where I did something wrong and in those days the cane was a tool they used on a regular basis, always remember when I was going to get caned, I remember wearing 2 pairs of under pants to lighten the blow, which did help I may add. I used to make the whole class laugh with my humour as the class clown. Hence not coming out of middle school with much to show for as education, but hey I had high school left to make an impression on my youth.

Onwards and upwards I am now eleven years old, moved up to high school, which was a massive level up to the third tier of my schooling life.

We all started as 2nd year students back in the 80's, 1984 I believe I started, with our long hair down the back and our most peculiar mullets, thanks to Jason Donavan and neighbours to give us someone to look up to in life. All the girls loved Kylie Minogue and Madonna, epic big hair.

Our school hall and reception area were as big as my whole middle school which was quiet daunting as a young lad starting out in a new world.

We coped very well, I always remember one lad in my class called Michael Jackson. On our first day of school, the teacher went around the class asking us to introduce ourselves, myself as Darren Fry, then it got to him, what's you name lad as he replied, 'Michel Jackson miss'. She said come on your not funny, and he had to plead his case that he was not lying, the whole class roared up with the laughter which was very very funny. Locking teachers in the cupboards were a few more tricks we got up to, but all was in good gest, schoolboy humour I suppose!

Again, not being very academic at school. I was amazing at computers, the old model BBC matters, with that trendy floppy disc unit at the side was always a favourite. I enjoyed computer studies the most, everyone used to ask me, yes me, to copy my homework, which I did only for the girl's mind!

Sports days were fantastic, we had a trip once a year to the proper running track, my mums job that day was raking the long jump pit for my favorite teacher, I was never in anything, cause I was always overweight kid, who was never sport orientated, but hey had loads of fun anyway. We had break dance competitions in our covered area with people bringing in their own music systems, we had a whale of a time.

We set fashions by breaking the rules wearing our chino trousers to school to be as cool as we could.

Getting to the end of high school, Saturday January 24th, 1987, I was coming up to the age of 14 years old. It ended up being the worst day of my life. I was close to my birthday and being a Saturday I was helping my father on his rounds doing grocery deliveries in Epsom, my nan was ill with a bad blood condition, always having blood transfusions. At 12 O'clock that day went to the phone box in the old peoples home, my nan was ill at the time, I rang my mother to see how my nan was getting on to see if she was getting any better. And bang was hit like a truck at 100mph to my despair was told my Nan had lost her fight with life and died at 78 years old. She was nearly 79 or would have been if she had lived another month or so. I was absolutely devastated and that when the trouble began for me. I cried solid for weeks and weeks, not being able to sleep. Sleeping with my mum and dad to get some sort of comfort, to this tragic disaster that just happened in my life.

Continuing with my schooling became very disturbed and different at school for obvious reasons.

In the days we finished school at 16 with an option if you got good grades to stay on to sixth form, which unfortunately I declined due to not getting very good exam results in June 1989.

June 1989, I left school, god knows what I was going to do as a job career. I knew I would join the YTS training scheme and become a trainee car mechanic. The YTS training scheme for anyone that doesn't know was a scheme to get the young off the dole and into some sort of job training scheme, set up by Margaret Thatcher. The pay was an astounding £29.35 a week for the first year and £35.00 a week for the 2nd year. Fantastic I hear you cry, which meant you did a day release scheme at college once a week. So off I went, left school the cocky little 16-year-old thinking that the world owed me something, top of our tree at school, to the big wide world of work, or trainee car mechanic as I chose to be my path. I was still badly grieving the loss of my Nan who I adored as was so close to her.

To go into a training course in computers, I was advised by people in my friend and friends of family circle, that if I want down that path, I would end up with square eyes by the time I was 30.

So, I went to plan B and persuaded the car mechanics option on YTS.

Great I thought a trade, always need cars don't we. Wrong, it all began with me leaving school that cocky young lad who knew everything, wrong. I was placed in a garage in New Malden a very well-known establishment at the time, which is no longer there. As a budding car mechanic trainee of course. It started great, learning how to mop floors, make tea, the usual apprentice stuff, we all have to start at the bottom. We know, but when you try to fit in with older men and try to be the garage clown. You start to get knocked down a peg or two or three. Beginning with the old jokes, could you go and get me a long weight from the stores, me being naive I was sure getting a long weight that I wasn't expecting. Then it continued a left-handed spanner was the next thing to peruse, knowing now it doesn't exist.

Then one day a car accidently fell off the ramp to having so much grease and dirt on the underside of it. I was then told 'oh dear you are gonna have to pay for that', me being that naive lad, who took most things at face value. I left to go home that evening after a long day worrying my head off that I had to pay out of my fantastic wages for a new car, that left the joke going for a long time, which really got to me. During this time other horrible things went on, like them wiring train detonators to a car, nearby was a bin which when I was told to empty a bin from the garage into one of the big industrial bins, which I did, opened the bin to a massive bang. My ears rang for days causing me lots of distress and I was anxious for days causing me sleepless nights. I complained to my College about my placement and the bullying I was receiving, I was moved to another big garage, which unfortunately meant, I left the frying pan and went straight into the fire, this place was unfortunately worse. Having the jokes of you must clean the floor with a tooth brush, I believed it all being that I was a young trainee, which everyone had to mock. So, the bad stuff just got worse and worse, jokes getting worse and worse. In the end along came a horrible horrible time in my life, I wanted to sue the two garages involved for the horrible action that had occurred to me, which my mum and dad advised me not to because you never beat these big companies, so my sleep and worrying just started to escalate into a big fat mess. I sat up all night writing fact by fact on what they had done to me, these grown men who acted like animals towards me.

This is when the mental illness grew, me getting violently aggressive towards my parents, neighbours, I would be playing loud music, full blast was annoying everyone in my wake, threatening people. I remember going shopping with my father to Gateways, a well-known supermarket at the time and having a go at random people for no reason, the incidents and the garages were really taking their tolls on me. Nobody knew what was happening to me including me, aggressive behaviour, being horrible to everyone just wasn't me. When it got worse and worse no sleep, the crying over being bullied, the awful experience that I had gone through just got worse. Then one day my mum said we need to call the doctor, I hated going to the doctors and have a real bad fear of needles and injections. So, when the doctor was called for my erratic behaviour, doctor came with his tidy little black brief case, they used to carry around with them. I started really freaking out with my dad's pick axe handle in my hand, no one was coming to my house to treat me, oh no. So worried that my parents were, the doctor came to the house to no avail, my mum and dad were forced to call the police on an emergency saying I was an irrational maniac and in a very bad state of mind.

So, seven police cars came screeching up to our lovely 5-bedroom house in a very sort after area, well it used to be until I started my antics. They all arrived wondering of course what the hell they were going to arrive to. Splattered brains all over the walls, no of course not!

A young lad of 16 scared of what the hell was going on in his head and what was going to happen now, as I mentioned before I wanted to sue the company's. So, the police arrived and had a chat with me, convinced me to put the pick axe handle down which I did comply to. They said that we will take you to these garages to have a chat with these horrible people, who have bullied you and turned you into this frightened young man who hadn't got a clue of what is going on in his head.

So off I went in a police car thinking I was off to these garages for the police to give then a slap on the wrist or more, but no wrong again I was taken to a police station instead. As a smoker at the time, smoking very heavily at the time and drinking, I was taken to be questioned, got a bit annoyed as you can understand bring told one thing and something completely different happening. So, becoming a bit argumentative I was put into a cell, given my cigarettes but my lighter being confiscate which was not a nice thing to happen, when I was frightened, nervous and a chain smoking scared young man.

So, hours later I remember a psychiatrist being called to assess my mental state, which he did, still frightened out of my wits. I was sent away to a hospital, to a notorious ward, called west part hospital because they had no idea where to put me. I ended up in Drummond ward which was full of old men, who had been institutionalised in there for probably ages. At first when I arrived I was interviewed in a room/office by this beautiful young lady, who I presume was 'the boss', she said to me you don't have to worry about anything, me being a young versatile man was pleased when she said that to me. Don't worry young man you can stay with me tonight I thought all my Christmases had come at once.

Oh my god this was great I didn't have a lot of interest from the fairer sex at school at any time really in my adolescent life. She suddenly said I had to go I am afraid, slammed the door, this massive door to a locked ward. There I was in this hospital full of mental patients, scary or what, was an understatement, I remember looking in to the day room, with the TV on and the TV programme was about suing companies and cooperative cases in the workplace. I was getting more and more wound up because I obviously didn't what to be there a moment longer. I was a big chap at the time, I thought I could fight the world and the world owed me something, which obviously it didn't, but to convenience a frightened 16-year-old this was a different kettle of fish.

So, smoking at the time, which hence in the 80s was allowed on the wards in hospitals. I was handled with old scary men, hassling me for fags as they put it, going to try and get peace in my room was not an option because they used to tap on the pipes, and I was a complete nightmare. Me being cocky and feeling like I was untouchable started being really cocky with the security guards, calling them black bastards which I know was an unthinkable thing to say, so I was getting more and more frustrated being there. I was getting more and more violent because consequently I would not go to bed. I remember it being really late, so the security guard was getting more and more frustrated with me, called his mates on his walkie talkie and 6/7 of his 25 stone black security mates came up to the ward then asking 'are you going to bed?' I replied get fucking lost you idiots or words to that effect. So then what happened next, well I was bundled into my room with me kicking and fighting then pushed 3 of them off of me but to no avail, unfortunately I lost the battle and had an injection straight in my backside and all I remember after that is waking up feeling like I had slept for a whole week (that is what drugs do to you). Obviously, I hadn't it was probably only like 8 to 10 hours, which was the first decent sleep I had probably had in about a week. Luckily for me I was moved that day into a more, let's say decent hospital for people, who were not so bad as the people which had been in Drummond ward for years.

So off I went to a different hospital a ward called Elgar ward, which was like heaven on earth compared with the last experience I had not 2 plus hours ago.

So, during this time I forgot to mention I was sectioned, which means you must be hospitalised for a minimum of 4 weeks in a mental health unit to be treated and made better, that was the plan anyway. So, O met some fantastic beautiful nurses, who were ready and primed to make that journey of recovery with me. I got showered by nurse's cos I was so drugged up and sedated I couldn't do it myself, no complaints there. I was on Chlorpromazine, definitely calmed me down, let's just say I was probably a zombie for a week or so. These drugs were so strong I could hardly move, sitting in a chair not being able to move isn't much fun I can assure you of that.

I was in hospital with young, old, middle aged people with all sorts of weird and wonderful conditions, all to do with mental health of course. People with alcohol, drug problems, people who spent too much money or people like me who were just victims of being bullied in the work place, being hit with a load of grief due to the loss of someone, not just someone, my best companion in the world, my Nan.

The drugs I was on sent you into another dimension, delusions come to you, a delusion is like a dream but you are awake, and you can remember everything that goes on. One of my many experiences is that I believed I could control the weather, I believed I was Jesus Christ standing in a small room, which in them days was the smoking room in hospital, which you don't have these days. I stood by the window seal, windows being closed of course because of security.

Believing when I blew out the wind blows, when I cried it rained, when I was angry the thunder came, when I was happy which wasn't that often the sun came out. Bearing in mind I was admitted late in the year, so the weather was not very good at the time I was admitted. My first real breakdown was coming to head with awful delusions. The only way I could block out the world, which I wanted to do is listen to my personal stereo, Walkman, MP3 players as they are called these days.

Robbie Williams music was my only get out, it was a release for me, his words meant so much to me. It actually was a comfort to listen so carefully to every word that was written by him or for him. If you listen to a song in depth not just listen but fully understand the meaning of the words and the story or a song or songs that someone has written it's like a story, try it someday.

The problem with me doing that is, I would sing the songs, while I was singing, out loud and among all the other patients, it cost me and my family a fortune in batteries to keep me going, oh and cigarettes. The albums and the words were my only comfort, I could reach out to his music and understand through his music what he went through with his battle with his mental health to battling with demons, is not an easy thing to get through, I can tell you that. Then while being in hospital I became a little obsessed with the music I was listening to. The delusions I was now experiencing were I believed I was Robbie Williams, I dressed like him. The long leather Jacket, the number shirts, which was a great fashion back in that time, the haircuts. No one could tell me I wasn't him, cos I believed it and with mental health anyone can tell you something, but you will never believe them because it's something you have in your head and no one can remove it. I believed I was in hospital with Paul Gascoigne, Gary Lineker, Gary Barlow, Michael Jackson (when he was alive) Jason Donovan, Morris Gibbs but they all had disguises on as in rubber latex masks on. Every one of my family, my mum and dad visited me every day and told me it was a load of rubbish, but you cannot convince a mentally ill person of anything. We believe what we believe, and no one can tell you any different.

I remember trying to escape from the hospital and go into town to a little-known haunt of mine which was called Chicago Rock Café and now it is called something else. I slipped out of a window, which word got around that was always left open at certain times of the evening. I had my slippers on from being on the ward, toddled down the road and got into the establishment. I had no money god knows how I got past the bouncers but did, into the bar I went, it was karaoke on a Monday, always remember that. I grabbed the mike off the singer/DJ and started singing into it, entertaining the people who were in there. Then I blagged a pint of lager off some stranger, was just going to take a drink from it and low and behold my dad just walked through the door and said 'What are you doing because if you got caught leaving the hospital and drinking alcohol whilst on medication, you would be chucked out and left to fend for yourself?'. You used to get breathe tested when anyone left the hospital, well those who were allowed, certainly not me I was on occasional observations at the time and managed to slip away without being noticed, but thanks dad you saved me from myself, good old dad.

So back to hospital for me that evening. I was one of those patients who wanted to play music and party all night, never sit in a corner, only when I was highly medicated, so I couldn't do these sorts of antics. I can always remember being told to get back to bed and the night staff saying please go to sleep but I couldn't switch off. We all wish we had a switch don't we, so we can just reset our batteries for the next day as It were.

Then I was coming to the final hurdle which I was becoming better, getting my sleep, which is the most important aspect to my illness, sleep equates good times and wellbeing. No sleep I become a party animal who wants to wake the whole ward up and have one massive rave up party all night long.

So like I said it was coming to the end of my 4 week period, I think I was in hospital for 6 weeks before I was able to leave after getting well again it was a relief for me and certainly my family, who visited every day I was in there, if it wasn't for the support I don't think I would of made it to 17 years old, So off I went, 17 years old, my brother in law at the time got me a job in ASDA, after the YTS went pear shaped for obvious reasons, I was so happy to get a job after my illness. I was employed as a produce assistant putting out he cabbages and apples was a good job enjoyed it a lot. Work was good I was full time and on ok money for a young lad enjoyed a year working there made some good friends.

Moving on to 18 years old, my sister got married on 2nd March 1991, I was asked by my bother in law if I would be his best man, I astonished at the time, as I only knew him for a few years, but he was from the midlands, so excepted to do this for him. But oh, the wedding went ahead no hiccups at the service or reception, I did my speech everything was hunky dory to use a better word. Then bang the mental illness reared its head for the second time in my life, dam thought I was cured. But oh no started drinking heavily, because of the whole pressure thing standing up in front of all these guests and doing the whole thing at a young age of 18. I was a very young 18, I lost 3 stone leading up to the wedding with the worry and the nerves, never told anyone just dealt with it myself and bottled it all up thought I could handle it all but no I couldn't.

Everyone said to me you will be fine, everything will be ok, but as a mental health sufferer you know words are just not enough to get you through the hardest times in your life. Talk is easy, actions are harder to put into place. So, 3 changes of suit size due to my massive weight loss.

After the wedding I was very upset that my sister was gone, left the family house, was a very strange surreal moment of my life, there was four in the family, now we were down to 3, so unfortunately the sleep deprivation started again, yeah you guessed it I was admitted again into hospital, same ward Elgar, 1991 not a happy start to my year.

Not sectioned this time, went in on my own free will, another 6 weeks in hospital to get me straight once again, I came out and I was put on Lithium which is a drug that was not very nice to me, I was very angry on that, wanted to fight everyone and I was very uptight, I used to throw lawn mowers around the garden when things didn't go my way.

Delusions came delusions went. I was so unwell I couldn't shave myself, I was so shaky couldn't cope with anything, Lithium at the time was a wonder drug that was supposed to be very good, but hey it didn't suit me. So, after 6 weeks of the doctors sorting me out, back to work. But I was not a nice person to be around on this medication, no sooner the word I was snapping at someone, a work colleague or someone fighting in the back. Years with a colleague in ASDA things calmed down a bit for a while. 3 long years I served at ASDA which were mostly good years. Then one day back end of 1992 I was playing silly buggers in the cold store with a few lads and we were all smashing eggs, with our fists playing rocky. We got caught when push came to shove, I took the blame for all of my mates and unfortunately that was the end of ASDA.

Then in 1992 my father took me on to work for him in the family business, working for him but not in a very good mental state I did very little work for him, with the medication I was on, I mostly slept in the van for most of the time I worked for him. Which was not a good part of my life.

In 1992 I got an interview at Sainsburys, which I successfully got the job as a produce assistant, same job as I did at ASDA as a full-time lad. Prior to getting the interview, I had massively piled on the pounds working with my dad, being lazy, my dad being very understanding of my illness, didn't tell me what to do let me be idle, I was a whopping 22 stone, which for me was a massive weight. I became lethargic and comfort eating became a very regular thing for me. Pizza became an evening treat for me straight after my mother makes me a wonderful cooked dinner. Eating was my get out and the only comfort booster I had in my life. So, one day I thought this had to go,

I was in a much better frame of mind and said right let's get this off, so off I went and joined the gym at the North Cheam, stage 2 it was called then.

So, this started in about 1993, the diet began, it was a massive marathon, I swam every day, went to the gym at least 4 times a week. It was a hard slog, but I achieved a massive goal for myself. I was doing something I really needed to do to make myself feel good. I came off the medication and things were looking good. I dropped 8.5 stone in around 3 years, I began thinking I was like professor Klump out of 'Nutty Professor', great film. Then I became buddy love. I then became very very special to the ladies, my god did I make the most of it. I became a very horrible person, someone who never had no luck at all with the fairer sex, to becoming someone who just could not stop pulling the ladies, I made up for all the years, I had not an ounce of luck to having all the luck in the world, things were looking good for that fat guy at school.

I became very lucky, so onwards and upwards, on to Sainsbury's. Started work there in 1996, back end of that year, got my head down and absolutely worked my socks off to become the best person I could be. Putting everything I had into the job, filled up the department like there was no tomorrow. I got really into the job and no one really worked that well, so I got my teeth into it and boy did I make a difference.

A supervisors job came up 6 months into me being there, so I thought hey think I will go for it, so I did, there was another guy that had been working there much longer than me, who also went for it think he had been there a couple of years, but he didn't really do a lot of work, a lot of wondering with the management and doing a lot of chatting to them and very little work. So, we both went for the same job, and guess what, yes, I got it, I got the job, I became senior assistant of the department, god did I feel good, sorry Jason I beat you to the prize. So off I went and became semi boss, I always wanted to do it. I had a lot of experience working with my dad, which I didn't do much, but taking a leaf out of my dad's book and watching him work hard, gave me that push to spur me on to greater things, thanks Dad! And all the experience I gained working at ASDA as well for 3 years helped me get started in my journey into the world of retail, which I did enjoy for some reason.

13

So off I went being a supervisor telling all these lads what to do, was rewarding, we really turned our department into something special, achieving lots of goals for the store, making takings back then to 1 million pound per week for the store, which was some achievement. So, after being there one year an opportunity came up to become assistant manager of the department in training, which was called an AMIT in those days. So against advice from my parents, telling me not to do it because of my mental state of mind, which at this time was fine, I was on no meds and was feeling on top of the world, my mother pleaded with me not to take this position, because it would be too much pressure for me and I could become ill again.

Me being me, pig-headed as usual went against their advice and low and behold I got the position I went for and was now a fully pledged assistant manager in training. One position below the manager of the department. So off I went into the big bad world of becoming a manager. I was successful at first, loving my new role, the job was running the department for my manager while he got on with more important things like paper work and ordering and schedules and all the important things of making a successful business. But oh no after 6 months or so of doing the roll, my training had to be completed with 6 months of getting the job, it was called our panel exam, which I had kind of left till the last minute, so in the end I had to squeeze 6 courses into like 2 weeks to complete my training programme. But unfortunately, things got very on top of me and the pressure built and built on me and I was in a classroom on a course and I started giggling uncontrollable and making very silly remarks in the training course, they didn't quite know what was happening to me. I was very high, due to the lack of sleep and worrying about all this training I had to complete in this two-week period, unfortunately I didn't plan my 6 months very well, i.e. do one course a month, I was too busy getting everything right and perfect on the department. So bang 1998 came with a bad bad episode, I was doing 15 hours a day at work, working 7am till 10pm at night, I just couldn't switch off from work, about everything, I used to plan my day in my head, what I was going to say to everyone in the morning, what I was going to do, Just could not switch off. I needed an on and off button on my brain, which unfortunately we have not got, dam! I did need one.

So, 1998 didn't start very well coz I was hospitalizes once again, to sort my sleeping and get back to my normal self. This was a horrible time for me because I thought I had failed in life and couldn't understand why this was happening to me all over again. What have I done to deserve this went through my head a million times. So off to Elgar ward I went for the third sitting in my life.

This time it was getting worse for me, I again was Robbie Williams as from before, but this time was very heavily into Natalie Imbruglia, well who wouldn't be with the looks and beauty and as her and Robbie had been through similar problems to me. I could relate to her, through her music 'left of the middle' was the album, that really inspired me, the words that were written in her songs really turned me in and tuned me out of all the horrible stuff that was going on in the psychiatric ward. There was some real bad stuff happening too, very ill people who just wouldn't leave you, alcoholics again, very ill people which kind of made me worse with the heavy medication which I was on, to slow me right down. I always remember my friend Micky coming to visit me on many occasions that he did, I was sitting in that same old smoking room, once again and I couldn't physically move from the chair being so drugged up my neck was to one side and chlorpromazine was taking its toll once more. He went off to get a nurse because he was so worried about me, because it was like I was paralysed, so in they came they gave me this drug called procyclidine, which suddenly perked me right up and I was able to hold a conversation with my friend.

During my mental health problems, I did not want to eat at all, all I wanted to do was smoke, smoke and smoke more that was my saviour or what I thought anyway. But we all know nicotine isn't the answer to every one of our problems, so this went on for a glorious 6 weeks (not) I had many visits from my work colleagues & I didn't hide my illness from anyone. I told everyone as you all know it is good to talk about mental health, get it out there, the more you bottle it up the more people do silly things like suicide, which was an option for me many times in my life, whilst sitting up all night, not being about to sleep is a horrible thing for the best of us, not only people with mental illness.

Sitting in my parents front room before being admitted, feeling pleased with myself all I want is to sleep, but whatever you do you can't switch off and the more people say to relax you will be fine, people don't understand you just can't flick a switch, so sleep deprivation is my main concern and my main evil to my illness/condition. So, I saw every doctor under the sun, while I was in the hospital, nurses were fantastic, helped me through the tough times. Oh, my if it wasn't for them and my wonderful family visiting me every day, I wouldn't be here today writing my story!

So, the episodes came, and the episodes went. I even had time to squeeze in a girlfriend while I was in hospital, which my mate Mike, always remembers him saying to me, only you could pull whilst having a mental breakdown, only you mate, how do you bloody do it, he said to me. So, I was getting to the end of my time in hospital and getting better thank god. Came out and went back to work, unfortunately I had to give up the whole management thing due to the stress I couldn't unfortunately take it, or for a better description deal with it in a manner that most people take for granted. So, I then became just an assistant again back to the bottom of the food chain for me! Which was good because the pressure had left, I became that small cog in the big wheel again which I was told every company needed, but it did not make me feel any better though. I believed I failed my company, myself and my self-esteem was knocked so hard, but I carried on and braved my demons. Basically, I got on with it, which you had to do.

So, 1999 arrived with a bang, no wait for it, yes, you guessed more problems, I decided to change my job and became a security guard working for a company. The security they used in my workplace Sainsburys. Me thinking the grass was greener on the other side, went for it, dived in with both hands and went on a course. Things were looking ok-ish, when I did the course, 3-day course, things went ok. Got placed in Sainsburys, first few days so far so good, then the pressure of keeping an eye on everyone and following shop lifters about, seemed like it was too much for me, once again, doesn't seem a pressure job really, but your brain is on the go 24/7. Keeping alert radio contact all the time and at the store there was plenty going on all the time, it was a nonstop job, keeping me on the go all the time.

So, I became ill again not being able to switch off and relax when coming home from work, my mind still racing and then the no sleeping for a week is like a boulder going down the hill, once it starts you just can't stop it. So, the admission to hospital was there again rearing its ugly head once again, yet another episode to deal with for me and my family, horrible stuff but just have to take it on the chin and get the hell on with it.

So, my episodes were slightly different this time, I was weirdly saying words like tap and then repeating backwards, so pat then I was saying pop and pop, I had a game in my head which lasted a long time, trying to find words that spelt the same forwards as they did backwards. Cat became tac, my dad's name Bob worked. So, this probably went on for a while, but I was shouting it out loudly for every other patient in the hospital to hear, which was not pleasant for them. So this time I was in hospital with tom cruise, well not really, a nurse that I thought was him in my head and in my world only fantasy is the only thing you have when being mentally unwell, you make your own world really, to become distant from the real world that you are struggling in.

So, drugged up more and more by the doctors. Slowly and slowly more up to become the zombie I was so used to being at this time of being in hospital. I can remember being shaved by a nurse, a male one at that because I just couldn't stay still and had no confidence to carry out a simple duty of shaving myself and having a bath wasn't easy either when you can hardly move, whilst being so out of it on medication.

So, I got bathed by such a lovely Irish man called Pat, he was there for me every step of my horrible journey of my mental state of this time. This time I was a quiet good-looking desirable chap and got friendly with this guy called Justin, he had been travelling to the far east, always recall having dinner in the hall down stairs and his sister came to the table. Me being me started to chat to her very good-looking young lady, one thing led to another and ended getting the guts to ask her out. Not on the first occasion, probably her 3rd or 4th visit to see her brother, it took me a little while to pluck up the courage to ask the question 'will you go out with me'? Then I thought how the hell am I going to take her out when I was locked in a psychiatric ward. Whoops never thought this through very well. Anyway, it came to me after a couple of weeks being in there and progressing and getting a wee bit better. I had some visit days which was like a day release scheme, which got you getting used to the outside world, for a few hours. So I used my day release to date girls, well you have to have your hand in front of you. So always remember her coming round my house sitting in my bedroom with me, me thinking god I want to kiss her but as you will know it, may not know when you are on medication a lot of it, you have the driest mouth, like the bottom of a buggies cage, so that was out of the question, just couldn't get myself to kiss her, because I was so embarrassed, to carry our this simple task of kissing this beautiful young lady. So, we just sat there looking at each other, like a couple of wall flowers, so that was the end of that short-lived date, not you, but me. That old cliché. So back to the ward after my little day release disaster. I became lazy didn't want to do anything, stayed in bed a lot not wanting to wash, not wanting to do much and if you are a sufferer mental illness you know what is the road to recovery, because you have been brought down from the highs and bought back down to reality and then when you start sleeping too much, you know the meds are working to much and hence you are becoming better and better each day. So, this was the case with me anyway.

I had a guy that slept on my ward, an old man named Sid. He was asked by me every day, if he could put my socks on, because I tell you what when you are so drugged up, is a very difficult task. Let me tell you that a. you fall over, b. you have no balance to even attempt to stand on one leg to carry this simple task that we all take for granted being well of course. So, this carried on for a few more weeks being locked up in this ward with a lot of sick people. Eventually when the magical 6 weeks were up, I was discharged and on my merry way I went. Then of course that isn't it, you must go to what's known as out patients which is where you are seen every

2 weeks or so as a follow up, when you are out of the hospital. So that was the end of that venture as a security guard life, was just not for me, so we moved on to the next stage of my crazy life.

The millennium came, celebrated round my best mate Jeremys house, it was a very good night, but at this stage I couldn't go out because after being ill, you don't want to be in public places I couldn't stand being in a night club, or anywhere I just wanted to be at a house party for which I saw it in with friends.

My friend Jeremy was there for me all through my horrid time in hospital, he visited me all the time, helping me, shaving me and just being there for me. I am so lucky to have friends and family around me because I know if I was left to my own devices, I am sure without a doubt I would not be here right now writing this book. So, after all that we are now in the year 2000, not much has changed but they live under water. Oh, sorry busted it like the year 3000 whoops. But your great great great granddaughter is still pretty fine.

We lived in a lovely bungalow at the time of this one it's the good one!

I believed opposite where I was in hospital, where all family and friends were visiting me. That a house was being built for me, opposite where I live on the wong gas sports ground, well it was quiet a good invention. They were building the house underground, so I couldn't see it until I came home. Basically, there was a tree there, that you pushed when you came home. What happened is the house which was underground completely flipped around out of the ground on like a swivel plate which was made of iron and when I came home as like a big surprise for me, you pushed the remote control as well, for your house to appear when you got home, or you could just push the tree for manual access. Well the remote was the sky controller, you used it as it was multi-functional. You pressed all buttons for the underground garage to come up, which had my 6 cars in, Ferrari, Lamborghini, Monster truck, BMW convertible, American Corvette of course black, with the big wings on the bonnet. Sorry got carried away with that one, what a beaut of a machine, that was.

Oh, dont forget the Audi Q5 for the wife ha-ha.

I was so rich in my awake dream, delusion in simple terms, not bipolar terms. I mean our world is a little trifle different to a normal person's imagination, so that was that button on the remote. Then you pressed on another one and all the curtains drew themselves in the house, I think you can get them now a days. Then you pressed another one and your swimming pool came out the ground also, so you could sort of hide your house away, when you were out, a bit like thunder birds I suppose back in the day. Then another button would bring your robot to get your dinner and wait on you hand and foot. Another one opened your automatic gates at the front, bearing in mind like a 20 bedroomed house, don't worry we had a robot cleaner, because he done nothing that boy, the boy done nothing, he never cleans up, you got the song, can I take that quote. Alesha Dixon. So, you kind of get the drift yeah. It was a fully automatic functional house. Bit like Alexia in today terms, but this moved everything and did it for you, not just answered your random questions and turned your light on and off and your radio. You had like a remote on your real car like remote control cars have, kids' toys, but this brought your car round for you from your sky remote. Crazy isn't it but the mind is a powerful toy!

It was December 31st of 1999, fantastic track by prince god rest his soul. We all decided to go to Mr Harris's house (Jeremys) they were having a little shin dig (I like that word sorry). Party I should say to all you young ones who would understand old lingo!

So off I went just getting over my last admission, couldn't go out and stand a lot of people after a hospital admission it took you time to break back into society gently as it were, so this first real outing out again, was my not like out of the hospital or the big house which I like to call it. So, it was lovely being invited by my best mate's family into their humble home, for what was going to be a millennium party. It was lovely to see all my friends I hadn't seen for some time, after being in Elgar Ward once again, being looked after by some real lovely nurses, thanks to my lovely nurse I used to call Mum, who nursed me to sleep like when I was a baby many times during my many delusions and bad time sobbing my heart out to hear that to everyone, Pat, Irish Guy, big guy loveliest guy you could ever meet and a guy called Jim Davidson which I thought was the famous one, oh dear how the mind works eh.

So, back to the party, thank you to Jeremys lovely parents to which I have known for many years for such a fab party as always. Mike and Caroline, Caroline is Jeremys Sister and a very good friend as is Mike her boyfriend. We worked together in Sainsburys during my dodgy time. Jeremy had a brother who is a lovely chap I met when I was 16 years old, who we used to hang around with in Charrington Bowl, playing cards with the Vince and dom the old school crowd. Playing the knuckle rap game If you lost, coming home with bleeding knuckles many a times boys will be boys I suppose. Mike was always there for me back in my 1998 admission, he took time out of his day to take me back to the hospital after I had escaped, which I did used to slip the nurses and just back to work to do my job because I felt I was letting everyone down and had to go in well I was admitted to hospital, so I ended up at Sainsburys, upstairs in the canteen with my line manager, saying to me 'Come on mate you have to go back, get yourself better, don't worry about this place', but what do you never say to a bipolar sufferer, yeah 'don't worry' it's just a waste of time. Sorry for people who thinking they are helping but generally it's a waste, but is a thoughtful thing, thank you. So, Mike bless him drove me back to the hospital and didn't like taking me back, but it had to be done for my own good and in the long run it was.

So, thanks to Jeremys wonderful family they have helped me out no end during my bad old days.

So, my journey was now back with working with my father in the family business, dad bails me out once again, but I was in a fresher state of mind thinking lots of energy and enthusiasm to make the business a much better and much more successful. So, everything was hunky dory, money was rolling in, I made the business much better, with new ideas, new structures and it was taking off to new heights, making a good future for ourselves. One of our old people homes that we delivered to in Walton, Neil Morrisey was filming, so was lucky to see him. And, during my time with working alongside my dad, he made me an equal partner, by calling the business R W Fry & Son, so I was on the way to succeed, once again things were good it was a good year. Also, were the news to follow and we were lucky to serve Mr Chris Tarrant and his lovely wife, Ingrid in their new home, before their split.

In this time I was trying to find that perfect woman that we are all searching for when we were young, but always when I got a date I would always tell these ladies about my condition a couple of weeks into the relationship and unfortunately 99% of them didn't like what they heard when I explained my problems and things that can possibly happen to me and they didn't last. So hence me having loads and loads and loads of short relationships and having lots of girlfriends and one-night stands became a lot easier and I didn't have to explain the mental health saga to them. So, had a great time holidaying with my mates Micky, loads of girls, was fantastic buddy love, was here and here to stay for now. Which was a great confidence boost after being so large and obese those years back and having no luck with the ladies, oh well enough of that!

So the business still going along nicely, was lucky enough to serve Nick Faldo's old house, one of my customers moved there and low and behold Elton John lived next door, never was lucky enough to meet him, but knocked on his door, they have these smart intercom systems on their door and you only get to talk to the maid/housekeeper but hey I tried. I was told we only use the internet for our shopping and get it delivered, so that was that. I loved chasing the stars, my dad always laughed at me saying 'One day sitting in our mobile shop, spotted bobby Davro drive past in his lovely merc, so I said blimey that was Bobby Davro, remembering his licence plate, I said to dad lets go and see if we can find where he lives, so off we went driving down all these random roads and suddenly we saw or I spotted his car on the drive and we sat at his house, talking to each other me and my dad, who was going to the door with a business card to canvas his house to try and get him as a customer. I knocked on the door a little

star struck, because I knew who lived there and he answered the door. I gave him the spill we are in the area looking for new customers, we have a mobile shop etc... Would you be interested, and he said, 'I will come and have a look at what you have.' We had a lovely display, tidied the van made the displays looking sharp and looking presentable, let's just say up to standards, so there he was bold as brass Bobby Davro standing there we didn't let on we knew who he was or anything, celebs like being treated as normal people, which is what we did he started eating raw mushrooms at the back of our van, then he started telling me and my dad jokes, think he was using us as a test, we laughed at his jokes. So one joke he told was at the time of bird flu being well known in the press, so he said god I was unlucky a bird pooped on my window I think he had bird flu, it was funny, very nice guy, so normal, which is nice to meet someone so down to earth thanks Bobby for the experience of meeting you.

So life was good, went to Cyprus in 2004 with my friend to visit his family had a great time, visited all the sights of Famagusta, was so nice spent 2.5 weeks there, had a girlfriend at the time, I had only know for a few weeks, she was a lovely girl got on so well, but after getting back from this holiday, I took her to Brighton for the weekend after all the late nights in Cyprus and getting up early, the drinking, the erratic nights not getting my regular sleep, I unfortunately had a blip. I was treated out of hospital and was lucky to stay out and not being admitted into Elgar ward. So was medicated by a team because I was still under the team and was seen by Dr Edwards, who was fantastic and controlled everything for me and kept me on my stable road which was much better than hospital. But unfortunately, my girlfriend couldn't get her head around the whole mental health scene, so I am afraid to quote another song, another one bites the dust, sorry Freddie Mercury using your song as a quote RIP man. So, on I went on the journey to find my true love and my soul mate. Then after my blip cleared up and back on the road to recovery met a lot of ladies that year, my god it was fun, but it was not regular relationships, weekends were fantastic, the Friday and Saturday nights, but weekdays were boring cause no one out in the week, so lonely times in the weeks. I needed that soul mate who I could depend on and help me through my horrid times.

So onwards and upwards health was good, business was good, everything was absolutely perfect, one thing missing love, or a regular relationship which I think would probably keep my feet on the ground and keep me stable, which I was yearning for so much. 2006 continued to look good, we moved to a new house, from our bungalow, along came 2006 things were ok. Oh, forgot to say I am a massive AFC Wimbledon supporter, football is my life, travelling up and down the country supporting my football team Wimbledon FC, which changed its name in 2001 and became AFC Wimbledon due to the unfortunate happenings of things that happened in Milton Keynes and the club moving and us moving to a new house halfway down the motorway. So a group of lads in a pub decided to set up a new club, and started from the bottom of football again from the combined county divisions, we slogged our way up the leagues and are currently in league 1, it only took nine years to smash all through the leagues and get our league position back, which was taken from us, that's the long and short of it, to save boring you too much about the whole football scene.

So, one day after a good win at the world cup in 2006 for Portugal, I decided to take my friends out to a certain rock bar called Chicago's, not there now. I remember the date very well it was Saturday June 17th, 2006. This day was a great day and the night was good, drinks were flowing, out with my friend Ken and his girlfriend Jane and his brother Billy, all getting rather merry and drunk. It was a regular haunt of ours and we knew a lot of people in there, so did my mate Ken. So, dancing to all 80's music and having a whale of a time, getting more and more merry. Celebrating the win for Portugal V Iran in the world cup, hey we celebrated and drink for everyone Portugal won 2-0. But hey football is football and any excuse for a good beverage or ten!

So whilst the evening was taking its toll Ken kept saying to me, I got this friend in here that I know who I want you to meet, me being very drunk 'yeah, yeah mate' and it happened like this, every time I was on the dance floor this particular young lady was chatting with Ken at the bar and every time I came off the dance floor for a drink he said 'have you seen her yet' I said 'No'. we were passing like ships in the night, he kept saying to her have you met my mate Darren yet, she was missing me too. So, at that stage it wasn't meant to be, until it got to a little before midnight, Bang, we finally met on the dance floor and probably walking into each other's paths, by chance or luck. So, she said, 'Oh you must be Darren' and I said yes, very short and sweet introduction and I always remember she pushed me up against the wall and began to snog my face off, my god, the song that was playing was Andy Williams, 'Can't take my eyes off you'. So, we danced to that and enjoyed a wonderful kiss, then at the end of the night, I was asked by her and her friend to go back to her friend's house of which I did. We drank back there at her house and we all crashed, me on the sofa downstairs with this your lady called Michila, we did get on very well, which seemed good, hold on fantastic had my luck changed? So, we all woke in the morning rather hung over and I started to get quizzed by her best friend, about my intentions to her best friend, lots of cheeky questions, like how much money do you have? Have you got your own business? Which I answered yes, to the first question was mind you own! So, then her friend gave me her phone number of which I had every intention to call the next day, as I told her I would do! But I didn't want to look too eager, I called her on the Monday gave her a day to sweat it out. So, then we arranged a date for the Tuesday night on which that day was a world cup football match and me being football crazy took her to a pub called The White Heart, its no longer a pub and was close to where she lived.

Previous of meeting her she tells me she lived in a cemetery which I was in disbelief, thought she was totally pulling my leg, but when I collected her for our first date, it was only bloody true. Her father was employed as a crematorium person who dealt with the dead bodies at the cemetery. So, I thought I better behave myself here or I could end up toast or cremated or something.

So, onto our date, I sat her in this pub in The White Heart which is not there now, on the level crossing. I sat her with her back to the big screen of which a world cup match was playing. So, whilst on the first date we got chatting me watching the football over her shoulder, just occasionally mind you, if you believe that you will believe anything. So, I started to explain about the old mental illness/condition that I have been blessed with. So, after the date I walked out of the place thinking well that's the end of that one! She knows now she won't be able to deal with that, so I told her about my last 4 episodes. So, she is aware, is she gonna be that 1% of people out of my 99% who can't and didn't stay around. So, we started dated things very very good and very explosive and I was on the top of the world, I was happy, very happy for the first time in a very long time. My life was looking up!

It was in the Nov we all attended a firework night, which Fred Michila's father always liked to arrange, Bless him. We all took fireworks and had a shindig (party). So I went into the shop, which is not the holiday inn, it was the old garage, where they used to clean your car. It was the five-month anniversary of me and my girlfriend being together, so I thought I would go in this firework place they had kitted out, just sold fireworks, it was kind of a seasonal shop, carwash, they did everything anytime really. So, I picked the biggest rocket I could find in the shop to try to impress the family because I had only known Michila five months and I can remember they invited my mum and dad and my sister and her boyfriend at the time. So, we had an enjoyable evening, sitting around the fire, which Fred had built, I think he was burning a lot of old wood, I think the three piece suite nearly came out also, anything would burn, he would burn it, you Firestarter you twisted Firestarter. His old wardrobe came out as well I think, old chairs, he kept the fire going all night, good job Fred and anyway we had all brought our fireworks. All Michila's family were there, Uncle's and Aunties, etc.

So, we all started letting off our fireworks and I was really bigging up my rocket cause I thought it was gonna be spectacular and the best because I was quite competitive, or I still am for the price I had paid, and the size of this rocket I thought it would go to the moon at least ha-ha.

But the moment came all the other fireworks were loud, banging, screamers, mine went up into the air very quiet and then got up really high and sort of fizzled out and didn't really do anything. I hadn't known the family that long and let's just say every family occasion all the rockets get mentioned, normally by Andrew who I might add is a Tottenham football fan, well what can I say, but it sticks in my mind Uncle Martin and Andrew looking up at the sky saying 'Well I hope your relationship with my niece goes better than your rocket son and don't fizzle like that.' It was a had to be there moment, thanks for the memories Guys.

So, the dating was going great, 2007 came so we had been together for a year, it was fabulous. We were getting on so well after Mum and dad buying this very small bungalow, downsizing and getting a smaller place and getting a good bit of change after the sale was very well off. But mum and dad being really kind and generous people, they wanted to see me and my sister benefit from this spare money they had. By paying my sisters mortgage off and with this bungalow we have moved into having a great potential. I had this idea of building a granny flat as it were on the side of my mums, I spoke to Michila about it, as things were moving along very quickly and was fantastically brilliant, if she fancied building this large side extension for us to maybe live in. Just an idea I said, she seemed very interested. So, first things first we put all the relevant plans and permissions to the council and went off on our first holiday together to Portugal for a week to think things over and have a great time. Which we did very good holiday, very enjoyable at one stage during a night out in Portugal sitting in a pizza joint after getting the munches after a night on the cocktails, we decided to have food, so Michila suddenly said god I need to use the toilets to words of the effect. So, this place had a front entrance and a back entrance, so she just got up walked out the back entrance and went to find a toilet. So, I am sitting there eating and enjoying my pizza, I am thinking god she has been gone a long time, 10 mins went by then at least 20 mins went by seems like forever. I was thinking I won't go looking for her because she knows where I am and where she left me and suddenly, she turned up, thought I had lost the love of my life, my heart skipped a few beats, that night that's for sure!

So that was that we had a lovely holiday. We got back, and my best friend. Jeremy, asked me to be his best man, I accepted with great pleasure to do this for my best mate. My mate who I had known for a decade, ten years wow! So was a little concerned about the pressure of being best man after what happened in 1991 when my sister got married, on March 2nd, 1991. So, this was on the back of my mind, worrying if the mental health was going to rear its ugly head once again. So, we did the stag do without a hitch, which was a pretty dam good night. Michila was there for me, to help me through the stress because it was quiet a big thing to take on. I was on regular medication at the time to keep me on track. This was risperidone which was a good drug. So did this big speech at the wedding which was quiet long, cause I got all these old pictures of Jeremy from his mother without him knowing and made a book up of say 8 to 10 photos. So, then I made a story up for every picture and as he was in the army at the time, one story I did was were in the army now, then one of him in school uniform, I did schools out for summer etc... you get the gest! It went down well so far so good.

I lost a lot of weight leading up to his wedding, cause I had put on a bit after meeting the love of my life, so I guess I needed to slim down a bit anyway. I think my suit needed resizing a good couple of times if not more. I had got through it without a hitch, with the help of a fantastic woman by my side, planning, cutting, sticking and helping me organise everything. So, it went ahead without a hitch. Which it did, until, Jeremys Father put a glass of red wine down quiet close to me at the top table of the reception and me being me I knocked the full glass of wine down myself all over my beautiful blue and white waist coat, what a disaster I thought, nothing what a bottle of white wine didn't sort out, it got rid of every drop off of the wait coat. So, what a day that was 28th July 2007, my best mate getting married to his soul mate Charlotte, love you both.

So, we carried on with that year, what a good year and somehow, I managed to escape the hospital, after the pressure, best man duty, blimey I was amazed.

So, we were making plans for our next project which was our extension, late 2007 all the plans for our new adventure had all gone through.

We all decided Jeremy, Charlotte Michila and myself to spend it and see the New Year in at a theme park. So, it was Dec 31st, 2007, funny enough new year fell on this date every year. The hotel had not long been opened and we though hey why not give it a whirl, like you do, we all love to try out new places, don't we. Well it was a nice place for sure we took a few cans with us like you do and got rather a bit silly quiet early on, because we did have some pre-drinks to say the least, Carling for Jezza and Kronenberg for me. We do like a beer or 3. So we were in the room enjoying the niceties of this fairly new hotel, we were having a lovely meal by a cosy beautiful open fire it was lovely, if you can set the scene, a big open fire, a cold winters night, great food I thought it was a little expensive for what we actually got, I like to fill my belly and be kind of satisfied, so I wasn't sure we were probably trying to soak up the 8 cans each that we had necked when we first arrived. On to the eve, there was a function room we were going in and out of, dancing and generally having a dam good time.

Until I tripped over this rather awkward situated speaker which was on the floor, well we were a little excitable that evening due to the alcohol that was running through us. We were kissing each other, Jeremy and myself were cuddling, pretending we were together, just generally being two lads that had the greatest of friendships and a bond you will never break even, if you tired with the biggest pick axe you could find. I might add, so getting back to the trip incident. I went over on my proverbial, my bottom, feeling rather embarrassed, I got up so fast like you do and I thought, or I hope no one saw, but unfortunately the doorman did. This big door man came bounding over and was very rude saying you lot need to calm down a tad, you are way to lively and are having too much fun, slow down don't dance like you are doing. Anyway, Jeremy who was an ex-forces ain't really taken kindly to those remarks and the way he said them, and we were all a little argumentative at this time of our lives, males locking horns kind of thing. I was a doorman at the time, where I met a young lady who was helping in the bar. Who later down the years became my friend Cam, fiancé In August 2018, sorry rambling again. So, you can understand Jeremy and I could look after ourselves, if push came to shove, which unfortunately it did with the rather overzealous, trigger happy bouncer/doorman. Well we got into an altercation, which got heated because for some reason us men never back down, it's a power thing I think, the stags locking horns again, trying to win our territory men eh! So unfortunately, we exchanged our not so niceties with this bloke and unfortunately being New Year's eve the local constabulary, well called by the hotel, in case it bolted up into more of a situation, which I didn't think it would, but being a public place I suppose they did what they thought was right at the time. But they were over cautious, so the police arrived and had a good chat with us and got both sides of the story, like they do.

One of the policemen said 'I recognize you and that tattoo you have on your arm, which was my football badge of AFC Wimbledon. I said no, he said Yes, I have definitely stopped you before. No, I said innocently no don't think so. He said yeah you have that big black 4x4 pickup truck, I said yeah, I have stopped you because I was dating Michila who lived in a different area at the time and I was driving back and forwards three four times a week and come to think of it I was chased by a police van because my truck had privacy glass you couldn't see in what so ever, it was blacked out all round with the darkest shade you could get, illegally I may add in the front side windows. They stopped me on a Crossroad by a Tube Station, I was driving to the cash n carry in for my business, my mobile shop and they came bounding down the road in there van full up with about 6 police officers, they all jumped out like it was a raid. I was on my own bearing in mind. They opened all the back-passenger doors and at the front and it was just me. I think they was expecting to see it full up with people smoking the ganga but no it was just me, minding my own business, I think they thought I was a drug dealer ferrying backwards and forwards, but they couldn't have been far from the truth, If it smacked them in the face. I went through quiet a spat of being stopped by the police at this time of my life, but I was 33, not into the whole drug scene never really was, dabbled when I was sixteen with a bag of hash, but that was about it, not a big spender when it comes to non-prescription from that. So back to the theme park hotel, we were kindly asked by management and the police if we could spend the rest of our evening back at our room which we did, saw the new year in there! It was quiet late anyway, so it didn't spoil our evening when you have distinguished marks on you like tattoos how people remember you. But it doesn't make you a bad person may I add. So that was that a great break was had by all, apart from a small storm in a tea cup.

My dad paid for this idea of mine to happen and early 2008 in the January after Christmas in came the builders Jan 6th. It was all going to happen a new place for me and the girlfriend to start our lives and our journey together. We had been together just over a year and a half, thing was flying, plans to move in together. Things were certainly cooking in my kitchen Baby. Our builders came in knocked down this old garage and room, that was on the side of my parents' abode. Great it was going so well but being woken up at 7am every morning by builders, parking in my drive waiting to start work at 8am, eating there breakie right outside my bedroom window, because you couldn't start your cement mixer to make any sort of noise till after 8am. So, these early mornings started taking their toll on me waking early every morning and stressing about everything that was going wrong and yes things were going wrong. The wet wet weather of them trying to dig big holes to get the footings sorted for our new place. We have a mud heap as big as a buffoon in wales. Outside on our front driveway the rain came, and more rain came, was so scarred we were gonna get crushed under this mud if it slid down, but thankfully it didn't but everything that could of gone wrong certainly did. Diggers getting hit, smashing into fences with the bad weather, broke a light on the digger. So the worrying started to happen for me once again over a couple of weeks of the early mornings, the building works going on and going wrong and all the mess and stress, yes you guessed 2008 wasn't good ten years from my last episode on the drug called risperidone, that drug was my friend for many years and great friends and family are my world, fantastic for a long 10 years, but unfortunately episode no 5 was certainly imminent.

So yeah I was doing the strangest things, this year, like the no sleeping again, the sitting up in the middle of the night, thinking please I just want to sleep please, with my dressing gown on, with the dressing gown cord around my waist sitting there in my mums front room staring at her chandelier thinking, I could just hang myself from these because of the frustration of a week without sleep. The boulder was going down that hill at 100mph, it's just I can't deal with this no more tears were there, the pacing up and down watching that clock all night, just the demon of not being able to switch that on and off button off on your brain or just pause your life and just sleep.

Everyone can tell you as much as they want to just relax, but you can't just turn on and turn off your emotions it just isn't that easy. I always remember the night my Michila was round my house, watching the brits to some music concert and Paul McCartney was closing the show and I believed I had to go in the bathroom, and I was next on to perform on the TV. Somehow my bathroom was backstage at this music event, don't ask me how, but what you believe when you are having delusions and what is reality are 2 somewhat different things! I was having my 5th mental breakdown, this was happening for real so that night after crying I was helpless, I woke my mother and father in the middle of the night and asked them to take me up to the hospital, of which they did, A&E at that time of night was pretty quiet probably 2amish would have been the time. My delusions at this time I had to be in a blue room because my head was telling me this and for some reason, I had to go into save the world. So, we sat up the hospital waiting and waiting as you do in A&E for the duty psychiatrist to come out and find out what the hell was going on this time. So out he came my mum and dad sat in this blue room, so in came the duty doctor me talking a load of rubbish, saying my drug has to save the world, you must give me a blood test so I can provide you with a blood sample to save the world, bearing in mind I can't stand injections one bit. I was asking for this, demanding this, so after the consultation from the duty doctor it was decided admission, no 5 was imminent. so, in I went to a completely different ward, now downstairs in Elgar still but they have had a move around. Which really through me because mentally ill people do not like change, we like our same routine, so off I was taken in there. I was really playing up being a pain to the nurses, so I was moved to a locked ward by this time hadn't really slept for a week or so, so the highs were becoming really high and me smoking was a lot at this time, kind of keeping me half sane.

So, this ward was ok, remember a lovely nurse called Noreen, who I knew previously from my previous admissions said, 'Come on Darren sit down have a rest' and at the time of being in this ward you were only allowed to go outside and smoke for 10 minutes every hour on the hour. Me still sat in this armchair must of somehow dropped off for like 15 minutes, woke up from this short and sweet little snooze, and was desperado for a cigarette, which I asked the duty nurse 'can I pop out for a cigarette?' and I was told 'rules are rules mate you have missed the window, you will now have to wait another 40 mins for the next opportunity. I went absolutely crazy because smoking was my saviour at this time and most of my previous admissions too. Huh, it was the time of the inside, smoking ban thing inside so the smoking room of as before, became an outside thing now! So, I am ranting and raving to the nurses, 'why come on please' I was saying only on deaf ears. So, walking down the corridor I was so mad I did a karate kick at the window not intending to break it, but smash went the big pane of glass, I was lucky really that the pane of glass did slide down and chop my leg off really, so I think someone was looking down on me that day. Previously to this visit to A&E I did visit the doctor (GP) and was told don't worry you are having a panic attack you will be fine.

But me knowing me and all of my previous history with mental health I knew I was heading for another mad episode, so while at the hospital a nurse came up to me, oh I didn't realise you had moved house, so had to go to a completely different hospital, which the ward was called Lilac ward, so in the morning I always remember this very young nurse, said I am going to have to take you in my car, ok I said not knowing me that well that poor young lady must have been scared out of her wit, an 18 stone big chap sitting in the front passenger side of her car I could of grabbed the wheel and done anything to cause damage to her or her vehicle, but thankfully I was not that why inclined at the time.

So off to a new ward completely different place not liking the change it hit me hard.

Previously to that my girlfriend came to visit me only knowing her for less than 2 years, was told by my family you have to believe what he says go with what he says do what he says don't argue with someone in a delusional state. So, she had to believe the complete twaddle I was coming out with, i.e. having to freeze my DNA to save the world if this DNA was put in to the time machine the world would come to an end and that would be the end of the world as we know it.

So with the arrival at this new venture for me, was very weird, threw a spanner in the works and completely put my world into a different dimension, but I got on with it because I had no choice to the matter, got to this hospital lots of people there, remember this big black guy sitting there with bruises all over his face sitting in this chair, he got up moved for a cigarette or something or another and I sat in his chair, he came up to me and said 'hey that's my chair I am the governor' as if it was a prison or something. So, I replied in a not very nice fashion 'Hey I am here now I run this ward all right you got a problem?' As he replied 'No mate your fine crack on' to which I did, the times I got hassled in there by other patients asking for spare cigarettes all the time it was like prison, cigarettes were the only trading you had. To get any in a place like this, while I was also in hospital the mayor of Kingston who unfortunately had fallen on bad time and had a breakdown, due to the pressure of his work, so it can happen to the best of us, no one is exempt from getting this awful condition. I think the statistics say one in three people get this mental disorder now a days.

So, in there I was, patients screaming in the middle of the night, some woman ranting about Eric Powell, saying speeches about how the blacks were treated badly, it was a frightening experience to say the least being hassled every half hour by the mayor, who wouldn't leave me along for some reason. I had to be harsh and hard in the end and just say 'can you just do one' but he came back and back. Always remember we were doing this puzzle in the big day room and every time someone came to visit me which I can add was every day the patients did a bit too, it was a massive project, I didn't have the patience to do it, I was busy smoking and running the hospital singing Robbie Williams and Elvis numbers, but my girlfriend visited every single day without fail. I was so worried after not knowing her that long I would be left by her high and dry and she wouldn't be able to cope with the whole mental illness state. That was harbouring my recovery majorly, so I was upset, and told her not to visit me and really, I didn't want her to see me in this zombie place. But she ignored my wishes and carried on which I am so in ore of her for doing this and she had to be so strong to see me like this and put on this brave face and front every day. My best friend Jeremy was the same he shaved me again during this episode to and was there for me so much. I couldn't have coped without great friends and family being there every day for me. I remember the drugs I was on and the high dosage and the toilets being quiet away round this ward, I couldn't control my bladder and I kept wetting myself on numerous of occasions, making it very uncomfortable for me and having a washing machine in sight became very handy for obvious reasons.

Then one day this happened again, nurse came in helping me do my washing because living at home I took it for granted my mother has always done my washing all the time for me, I was her little soldier boy, and I took advantage of this being a lazy 35 year old, yeah I know it's sad my mother still doing everything for me but most lads are the same. So, washing day the nurse helping, in goes my trousers all my other bits and bobs, in the machine and away we go, then suddenly oh where's my mobile phone? you guessed it the pockets were not checked, and it was in the machine, bye, bye phone. My sister in law Erika tried to claim it off the hospital through the nurse not checking it, to no avail in the end it was my responsibility also, so luckily my best mate Jeremy came to the rescue once again and lent me a phone which was a massive decent thing for him to do. So, I could have some sort of contact with the outside world, which was a god send. So at least I could phone the girlfriend and keep in contact with her and other members of my family because it's a very lonely place to be when you find yourself sitting in the chair watching and waiting for 2pm when visiting time started, hoping that the doorbell on the ward would ring for someone to visit you. But when your family were working and friends etc. visiting didn't really happen, but like 6pm onwards when work was done. So long days sitting in a place full of strangers all with different problems like alcohol abuse, drugs and the black guy who told me he ran the tooting posse and then the reason he got a bruise on his head is because he had a gun shoved in his face which caused this and a mayor who wouldn't leave me alone and an old lady who wouldn't stop talking to me and me just running away from everyone. I started smoking about 60 cigarettes a day costing my poor father a fortune supplying me with the habit. I was probably giving 20 a day away because I was a pretty generous lad, would give anyone my last penny if it helped them. I always used to find myself standing outside the nurse station which was like a small armoured box, which of course was locked to keep them safe from the patents, which I can understand they certainly needed a safe haven.

Tablet time about 9pm was always a lot of fun because my delusions at the time, was that we were on big brother not just me the whole dam ward and the outside world was watching every move we made, with exception of the toilets of course. So, the thing in my head was that there was camera around everywhere. The country was watching Lilac ward Tolworth hospital. I told a couple of people about our TV in hospital was set on completely different channels to what everyone else in the country was watching. So, I decided to set a new fashion of wearing my clothes inside out, jumpers' trousers, jackets some would say like my mum "what are you doing? "I would say "this is the new fashion I am setting everyone will soon be doing this.' I am the trend setter for the young kids well everyone and when I went into my private room that I had I was safe like my base, but I believed it was a secured lift. Which took me up a level if I stayed in my room for a few minutes. It took me to another level to which I had a view of from my room, so I came out my room and I was on a different level it was a little like the glass elevator from the film Charlie and the chocolate factory. I had to close my eyes and it was all happening by bloody magic, crazy and delusional now but by god I believed it all at the time.

So tablet time 9pm, I refused my tablet many days of being in hospital because I had it in my crazy head that someone was trying to poison me and kill me because I was the superstar on TV earning all this so called money and someone wanted my phone as that high earning celebrity on the TV which we know was a crazy delusional fictional thing in my head. So the nurse giving out the tablets was a dead ringer for Eddie Murphy, so I believed Eddie Murphy was giving me my drugs every night, which was quite an honour (oh dear how that mind works ah) Scary stuff so every night god bless Eddie Murphy for trying to make me sane and well enough to leave after I was convinced after a few days he wasn't a missionary trying to kill me, I buckled and took my meds, always remember one night I had all this pain in my bloody legs, probably from running around the ward like a complete high looney, he said 'Come in the tablet area I will give you a rub down' to which he did, so on went the cream and a rub down. Legs only I may add. But it felt so much better after it that's for sure. Bedtime there was cool because mostly we had sleeping tablets pretty much every night to give the night staff nurses a peaceful night, because when I was up all night and high I loved the world and everyone in it and just wanted to party and I mean party all night long, thanks Lionel for the song quote love ya and your music.

So many long days in there being on television every night took it out of me! Delusional fool, I hear you cry, but when us, bipolars believe something there ain't no one man or beast that can change the thing of someone is a maniac bipolar state. The quotes my poor girlfriend had to believe when my family told my girlfriend that my DNA was in the freezer, I had to save the world, my god I wonder to myself everyday why she didn't run for the hill. I will never know to this day.

It was the time of Shannon Matthews's disappearance all over the TV that was the time I was in prison (I mean hospital) well it was like prison, if you have ever experienced an admission into a psychiatric ward. My friend came to visit me Michael Young thank you. It was time I was not eating and would refuse food, because that's what we do, crazy human beings that we are and a funny story when my mate came into visit me, I remember saying I am not hungry mate you have my dinner, for which he did and bless him when he tried to leave after sitting hours, they said 'where you going sunshine, you can't escape that easily' thinking he was an inmate sorry I meant a patient, it was so much like I imagined a prison to be in a ward like this because everywhere is arguments, exchanging can I buy a cigarette off you all the time you were completely hassled all the time by patients, there was no rest bite. I can always remember my other friend Mike Spalding saying to me when I used to get let out for an hour of two and used to go back he used to say blimey Darren you are so much better when you are not in there, you go back in amongst all the sick people and you slip back into a lull. I became one of them again he said it was like 2 steps forward 2 steps back, thanks Paula Abdul for the song quote. So, I had to battle with not only the illness I had but everyone in there who was mothering me all the time.

My mate Jeremy was in the army a while ago and left at the time and I got it. I heard that somehow, he could fly a helicopter and he would take this helicopter out and go up there fly above the hospital and fire ping pong balls at me from the air, as a lot of fun cos he always used to wind me up, bless Love him. I think it was the pipes in my room for the heating or something used to this fringing noise. I used to think he is up there again using me as target practice again how the brain functions. My mum and dad as I said visited every day and my girlfriend, sister and her 2 Children. They liked to stagger in, so between 2pm and 8pm I have pretty much a full card of visitors for that 6-hour period, which was so nice and to be home if I didn't, I don't think I would be here to tell you my story. But you must remember you must talk about your problems to a stranger your family anyone that will listen, you must get your problems off your chest. Bottling up is a very bad thing your head is messed up and you start to do stupid things and delusions become a reality, which can be dangerous to your health, it makes you wanna fly sometimes to god forbid the unthinkable throwing yourself off a building or some hair strained crazy idea like that, which we all have those mad thoughts, but it's easy to say we all know 'pull yourself out of it' release but these easy actions are not so easy to follow through.

I recall my girlfriend missed one visit to visit me in 8 long weeks while I was on my little break, in Costa Del Lilac ward as I used to always refer to it as. So, my last couple of weeks being in hospital I was allowed to have what was known as day release, which is what it says on the time, a day release away from the hospital. Which was good to get out of the big house, then I used to come out to see how my extension was going on our house, which was coming on very nicely, roof was nearly on, everything was going well on the building front which was brilliant. But one thing I found was when you were out for the day, I always felt nervous and edgy, and found myself wanting to be back in the hospital which was very strange, think it was because you got used to living there for say 4 weeks you become sort of accustomed to it. It was weird being anywhere else like for example going for a walk with a nurse was a real treat around the grounds of the hospital. At the time I had a lovely 4x4 Mazda truck nearly new and being on medication I was of course forbidden to drive. Which really frustrated me because one of my down falls are manoeuvring my car. So I always remember on one of my day releases my best mate Jeremy saying 'come I will take you for a drive mate in your truck' and I know this may seem weird but that small thing was like my highlight of my week, something so small became something so great and it would take your mind off the rubbish that was going through you head even if it was only just a short 10 minutes spin around the block it meant so much thanks Jeremy, you help my rehabilitation so much.

Whilst in hospital I had to go to occupational health many time on my five admissions, so I used to go to music, play instruments, relaxation therapy, remembering that one time we all had to lay on the mats in a hall and listen to music and try and just relax but I was unfortunately in a high mood that day and started laughing uncontrollably, so funny that everyone in the room to which there was quite a few to laugh to, I was asked to leave that class cause I was putting everyone off.

So, I remember getting to the end of my admission, I had to sit in a big room with my mum, it was called ward round, to decide if you were well enough to be discharged from the hospital. There was about ten or so people in there ranging from psychiatrics to your nurses to doctors to a new appointed nurse who used to follow you around all day, your kinda of one to one to make sure you were ok. So, we all sat in this room and they would all ask you questions very daunting and frightening, it felt like when you were under interrogation. So I went on for 20 minutes or so in the end yes to go the green light by this time, I was officially given the label of being bipolar, yippee I have words after my name not nice ones I may add. So the different meds they had found for me were called sodium valperate this drug has been very good to me, it has been heavily talked about in the press that it is not good for pregnant ladies, it harms your unborn child, but hey its cool I am not likely to get pregnant, not this year anyway. So, with the title officially given to me I felt the doctors have actually got somewhere with me, even though I think I have officially had it since my first admission back in 1989 but it wasn't proven then because they thought I was schizophrenic at first.

So off I went on my jolly way out of the hospital to carry on with life in the big wide outside world, called life.

What is a delusion? An awake dream really (when you're high). I had the first delusion whilst in Lilac ward, well it was the time that little girl went missing, very heavily published in the news, Shannon Matthews, well here we go wait for it cos this is madness (baggy Trousers) sorry song quote ha-ha.

Well this is how it all started, I believed we were all on big brother and the whole world was watching us in the hospital, told you it was unbelievable madness, but that is a delusion, Frank Bruno when he had his breakdown he believed that he was Frankie Detorri and no one when you are ill can tell you it's rubbish cos, you don't believe them whatever they tell you. You are in the land of delusions it's a real thing for you at the time, its rubbish now you're well, anyways, I was the top celeb in this one because I was always the star of the show! No matter what, no back stage for me directing ha-ha or playing the supporting role at one stage, I turned my jacket inside out because yeah its true I was setting a new fashion, singing all the time in the ward, into their speaking glass, where the nurses used to lock themselves in their office for their safety, it was like a 30 x 15ft room, felt sorry for them really, they were like animals in the zoo protecting themselves from us the patients, bazaar but true. Young girls (nurses) used to run from one office which was situated at the other far ends of the ward. They came out but when I was there I was a big 18 stone guy, quiet frightening to say the least. Singing Elvis all day to them. Stuck on repeat mode. Blue moon was one number I love the colour blue, I smoke sky blue cigarettes Benson & hedges of course, blue moon earlier, episodes on breakdown so you get the drift, oh and blue Wimbledon of course, don't forget the Dons.

So back to big brother, cameras hidden of course, were everywhere in our ward, streaming live TV, yeah live TV all over the world, built like the Osbourne's, Sharon, Jack, Ozzy and sister don't know their names soz. So, the lightening panels I believed in the ceiling used to charge us all up, like a mobile phone. Rubbish isn't it, told ya. And we slept, we were like robots coming out to play ready for the world to see, funny how the MIND works isn't it. So, we were all on show and all celebs, think deep down I have always wanted to be a celeb really, like the Robbie Williams connection, I am now obsessed with him, which you may think! It's just therapy for me listening to his music and all his albums, 45 Albums he has made to be precise and bipolar and also always precise and OCD, crossed T's and doted I's and all that. So, for the 6 weeks I was admitted for I was on the telly, so I hope that sums a bit more up for you!

So, got out and the extension on the bungalow had nearly been completed, few more things to do, roof garden, decking etc. I remember getting out around April time, I recall because my birthday was March 20th and remember my mate Jeremy buying me this rather smart jacket and everyone buying cool gifts all the family had and I was only allowed out for the day for my birthday, My Michila my girlfriend was also showering me with gifts which I felt very special and loved like always. So, I had it in the pipe line I was going to ask my Michila to marry me!

I was going to have a house opening sort of party when the building work was all completed and was going to go down on one knee, in front of everyone but I must admit I did bottle out on the idea, so I did it around a week or so before we had this party, got a ring beautiful it was just like my lady, got down on one knee in the front room and did it, luckily she said yeah, already been and asked her father for his permission or these days the green light as it were things we looking rosy in my garden again.

So, on the completion of the extension we had to buy everything to go in it because we had chosen everything in our project to our spec it was lovely or nearly, cause my builder who is also a family friend did give his professional input on where to have the bathrooms and kitchen etc. For the better I am not sure but hey that's all good it's built thank god and looks really beautiful. So, we have to buy all the appliance stuff from scratch, fridge, washing machine, oven, dishwasher, microwave the list went on. Not cheap but I had a little nest egg that paid for it all, so Michila moved in, engaged and everything we started our little lives together, which was fantastic living on one level. Bedroom at the front of the property, bigish lounge/diner. Loved it decorated all to our choices was good. Cause business, my own business was going good at this moment in time earning good money thanks dad for running the business while I had my little 6-week holiday, well if you think that was a holiday think again, far from it. So back to work fun to get my teeth back into work, which was good, I had to get back to some sort of normality, so Michilas mum and dad had a time share we were asked to go for a couple of weeks to Madeira with this on a much-needed holiday. We have just had a party of our own and Michilas Uncle Kevin had just had his 50th Birthday, which luckily Michila drove to, he lives on the coast which was too long for me to drive to. Just getting out of hospital a short while ago.

Previous to this Michila never drove when I met her, and she luckily passed her test just before I was admitted to hospital which was a god send for her to visit me all the time when I was in there as I said she missed one visit on one day over the 6 week period, I was there. That day she missed I always remember, her dad Fred was in poor health after having a routine operation and couldn't visit her sister's mum and her 2 uncles came to visit me that day, Uncle Kevin and Uncle Martin, whom I got on with like a house on fire. I remember it being pitch black dark and I said to them come and see my private room its nice, they came along and said 'Yeah its nice', I then pulled the curtain back because they were closed at the time and I said to them both 'what of you think of that view? They just looked at each other and rolled up laughing saying, I can't see a bloody thing it pitch black dark'. I can tell you they never ever forgot that cause from that day they tell the story of the room with a view, we can joke about it now. But I believed it to be normal all the time. Saying it, sorry went off track there. Back to the holiday, it was absolutely fantastic since eating nothing hardly while being in hospital and really big from zero to hero, from eating nothing to eating everything in sight and went on holiday in the August being the size of a house again. My weight used to go up and down like a bloody yo-yo, on tablets made you hungry, eat nothing being ill in hospital when you didn't want to eat at all, so it was a constant battle fighting your weight all the time which wasn't ideal, I went to weekly weighing sessions at the hospital to try and help me sort it all out but it was so bloody hard. So, in Madeira I looked like a proverable beach whale, I was probably back to the 20 stone mark again, which was good, but I think you get comfortable when you are in a relationship and not worry so much what you look like because you become in love and nothing else matters really.

So we had a beautiful time there with Fred and Pam, Michila's Parents, it was a break I really needed, we shut the business down for 2 weeks also, which gave my dad a well-earned rest also, which he needed keeping the business a float single handed which wasn't easy, cause we had both built it up to be very busy.

Its 2009 I was 36, things were looking rather Peachey for me, in love totally well, but fat again! So, a diet began it seemed like I was always on a bloody diet and I love my food too much it was a comfort for me in times of trouble, which was quiet a lot of my life. So 2009 arrived Michila got pregnant Way Hay, we are going to have a baby think she fell in the middle of June because I remember we was at a fancy dress party, good friends of my mates Jeremy, remember we went as characters from the film Grease, the girls as pink ladies and me and Jeremy as John Travolta of course, well a fat John Travolta on my part, So everything was brilliant baby on the way we were really happy.

But no bang we were hit with another stroke of real bad horrible luck, Michila had pains, oh no we thought what's going on, so we took her to A&E, we were all worried, went to sit in the cubicle, Michila was crying in pain and a stomach ache, she could not deal with the pain that's for sure the doctors came and examined her, but unfortunately very sadly we had lost the baby, she had a miscarriage and we were very distraught as you could imagine, our first chance of a family had been snatched away from us. It hit us pretty dam hard, but luckily, I escaped the realms of the dreaded hospital, the admission of my mental health I mean. So off we went home both of us feeling very very sad and distraught. So, the doctors started to find out why. In Michila's former marriage before she met me, she had lost a child also, so they began to investigate and investigate they did to found out that Michila has an under active thyroid, which she was then medicated for and treated. She had to take thyroxine for it every day and started the meds which became a thing she would have to do every day of her life.

So we carried on and on fastly approaching to 2010, we had been together now for close to 3.5 years, it was January 2010 the start of the new year, which was gonna be our year, I hoped so much for a bit of luck for a change would be nice, we were so desperate to have a child to make our lives complete and the memory of losing a child out of our system, you never forget a tragedy but it does get easier with time. So, January became an excellent life changing month because a trip down the chemist I believe for that lovely pregnancy kit in at the all-night chemist, because if I remember rightly it was a late trip for us because Michila was late for her period. So, we came back from purchasing our white kit and god was we praying for that little blue line.

So that evening being very late say 9pm or 10pm and remember we got home and did the ultimate test, with me praying whilst she was in the bathroom doing the necessary. Then she came out shouting and smiling saying oh my god I'm pregnant yes'. I said with a smile on my face as big as here to Kentucky quoting that chicken shop which I love. So, we started again the journey of being pregnant, it was always in the back of our minds after losing one child, so I literally wrapped her in cotton wool, phoning her all the time at work and was saying are you ok? You're not lifting anything to heavy, are you? She got a bit annoyed at me keeping on, think it was my condition that sometimes I do obsess about things and go a little over the top. Asking her if she has eaten her fruit, her 5 a day, me being a greengrocer she had plenty of choice of fruit, sitting on my front driveway, as a mobile shop was there at 24/7. We could have anything she wanted having a shop literally on our doorstep, which one of her mad cravings was granny smith apples and funny enough her mums maiden name was Smith, so maybe an omen that she liked granny smiths because her nan was a smith. Maybe a family thing who knows, so she ate probably 4 or 5 a day. I didn't make a lot of profit out of a box of those during the pregnancy of her craving then that for sure. So, heart burn became a real Achilles heel to Michila, so we had to get shares in Gaviscon (only Joking) but my she drank that by the bottle, just how she used to drink her favourite tipple Malibu and lemonade (no ice I might add).

So, 2010 was the start of a brand-new journey for us with a little person inside the love of my life. So, 3 months came our first scan because they had to keep a close eye on her due to the miscarriage only 7 months prior to this

47

pregnancy, which we were very worried all the time about it because of what had happened, which you can understand why. We decided to have a 3D scan which was really great they scanned Michila and we saw on the screen it was so beautiful to see a little miracle on the screen in such details we saw, its face was so clear on the screen the detail was incredible. So the nurse asked us did we want to know the sex of the baby, so we answered yes please, but unfortunately on the day of the scan they baby had its legs crossed, so the nurse at the hospital couldn't see what the sex was, so the nurse said I am so sorry we can't see today, the baby wont uncross its legs. So, she said you can come back for free because we had to pay privately for this scan and have another for in a weeks' time, so we did. This time it was successful, we found out we were going to have a beautiful baby girl and we were so elated, we came away with still pictures of the scan and a video of this to look back on it in years to come, to show her first boyfriend and embarrass her. So, on wards with this pregnancy, things were good right now happiness everyone waiting for that long 9 months to see the new baby born. So, we had a hot summer of 2010 remember Michila the granny smith version, me getting poorer with no profit on my apples that year (only joking).

So, this day came 16th October 2010, we were advised by people that a spicy curry would bring on the birth, so we went out to a restaurant for a curry, Michila being a korma girl was advised by the owner of the curry house to go for a madras, so that is what she had. That evening when we got home, I can recall so Michila was having a few twinges that evening we thought nothing of it, so we called the hospital stating that it was starting, but they said it's too early and see what occurs, so we did. So the labour was beginning, bang I think the curry worked, so we called Michilas Mum Pam and her sister Alana to come over about 4pm I believe, so we were all sitting here in my front room/kitchen and Michila was having pains every 20ish minutes or so and we were all sitting there timing on the clock on how apart they were, this one for most of the night, we rang the hospital they said its way too early to come in so we were told to come when the contractors were 5 minutes apart, but this process was slow, it went till 3am, still 10 minutes apart etc., so my best friend Jeremy always said to me 'Mate call me anytime night or day I am here for you no matter what' he always said, so I called in that favour and I think I rang him between

3 and 4 am in the early hours of the morning. He came over in his BMW x5 which he had at the time and very kind of him he took me, Michila, Alana her sister and Pam her mother who up the hospital. All night long Alana and Jeremy were there for me as support down stairs sitting in the foyer of the hospital. I was upstairs with my fiancée Michila and Pam her mother was chosen by Michila as extra support for her in the birth suite all night I was up and down stars, a bundle of nerves, my mate Jeremy being there for me, your outside smoking and he was there my rock to calm me down in my hour of need which was a god send that Jeremy and Alans kept asking if anything had happened yet, I said no all-night this went on for. Of which Jeremy was still here with me, Sunday morning came, Jeremey had to leave because he had a 6 month old of his own to look after, so I recall at 9am they gave Michila an epidural, which is a needle in her back I was so worried all night pacing up and down the corridors, drinking hot chocolate from the tea trolley in the hospital. So 7am epidural, I couldn't face seeing this, so Pam said to me she is in great hand with the doctors and nurses, so we decided to go and get coffee and breakfast in the outside cafeteria area in the hospital. So we left it about 40 minutes and went back up to be with Michila, still the contractions were so slow and nothing was moving, it got to 10am – 11am still nothing, then Michila was getting so tired and didn't have any more energy to push of which she was trying to do, just before 12pm they gave her, we believe too much pain relief in the epidural and she just was feeling the contractions as much and they were listening the midwives to her stomach for heart bears etc... They became a little worried and called in the doctor, just after 12pm to which Michila was pushing with all her might but nothing still, I was too nervous to be down the business end as it was, I was just holding her hand there were so many wires and machines in the way I didn't want to trip over and unplug something because I was so clumsy anyway. So, the doctor came and helped with the birth and at 12.34pm that afternoon on the Sunday, as the best thing ever in my life, my beautiful baby girl aimed to make my life complete and Michila was handed the baby straight away.

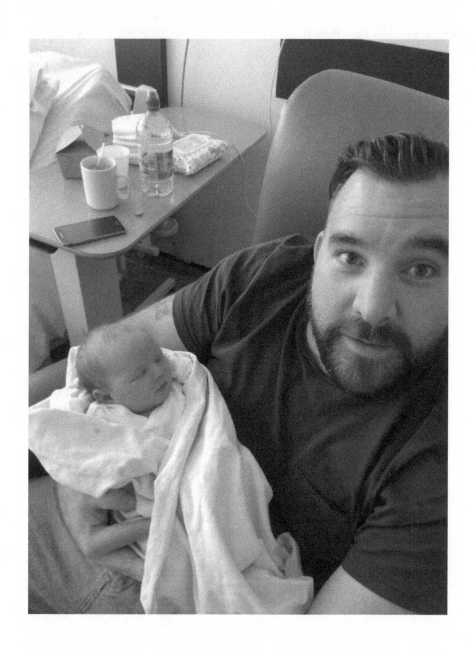

This beautiful baby girl who was perfect in every way this day I only dreamt of happening had become reality. So always remember leaving the hospital because Michila had thyroid complications she had to stay in until Sunday evening around 7.30pm. I had my 4x4 truck at the time and I placed my perfect package in the rear seats in the baby seat and got into vehicle to find myself driving and around 10mph down the road, never drove so slow in all my life, but to protect this perfect young baby if I could have wrapped her in cotton wool I would have. Oh, and don't forget the bubble wrap too for double protection. So, we got home with this young baby, oh and the hospital didn't give us an instruction manual how to work this baby and how to look after her! We were totally clueless as thousands of parent around the globe are with their first child, We all got home we all lived on one level ground floor extension of my mum and dads bungalow, they lived next door, we were totally separate we had our own bathroom, kitchen, like and granny flat really on the side, So we had support there with my mum and dad next door, but I may add we never really used their advice as we wanted to do this journey solo, just the three of us, so here we go buckle up and let the journey begin.

I had become a house dad by staying at home after Michila had 6 months off. It was down to me to look after this baby girl because I packed up the family business due to internet taking off, thanks to online deliveries, supermarkets. So, I decided in Feb 2011 to apply for Sainsbury's again after leaving previously after my breakdown in 1998. To which I was successful, Michila went back to work as a manager, I went back part-time, Saturday early mornings and one late night stacking fruit and veg on the shelf in Sainsbury's. So, house dad, I didn't have a clue nappies were not easy to do, quiet challenging to be honest. This little bundle of joy sure did change our lives that's for sure. We decided to have a christening in Feb 2011 her middle names we choosen after our nans, god rest their souls. So, the christening went off without a hitch all friends and family were there to celebrate this wonderful occasion. She was officially named and bought into the world, by the church of England also, registered as a little Christian too.

So, this was a wonderful occasion which I will never forget for as long as I live. So, everything was good the mental health was peachy my life was peachy this was so good. I couldn't have asked for anything more.

So after all this Michila and myself though we would have to make this official and tie the knot as it was after 3 years of engagement we decided it was high time we got married so, we set a date for the wedding to be confirmed as 2nd July 2011, we originally wanted it on the 17th June because we met on that date and it would have been easier to remember one date rather than 2. When we met and anniversary the same day, me being a bloke we don't like having to remember to many dates, just makes life more simple, like our species, ha-ha. According to a woman.

So, the preparation for the wedding began, Michila being married before, we couldn't expect her father Fred to pay again so we decided to fork out the whole cost ourselves of which we did, from the invitations to the church to the venue, the car the rings the hire of suits, food and everything. So we stated to sort the venue and what church, so me being as avid AFC Wimbledon supporter it was a no brainer, to have it at the football club, because I got a discount and b) it was memorable to have it next to the pitch in the club house or bar, which was right next to the greatest pitch of all where the best football team in the world plays, my Love for AFC Wimbledon. So that was sorted, date arranged, everything was in place, we went down to king's meadow the home of AFC Wimbledon to have a play with the tables and set them out to how we wanted to look on the big day, of which we did. The man said 'Yeah that's fine I know exactly what you want'. So off we went to sort out lots of other things, I was nervous and excited at the same time and of course was very worried how my bipolar situation, is under pressure, going to be too much? Am I going to crack under pressure or is a good women going to be the one thing I need to keep my head straight and my feet firmly on the ground! Only time will tell folks.

So, we designed all our own invitations well my fiancé Michila did she was much more arty than me and brilliant at designing the prefect invitation, they had to be looking pretty damb good to. Thanks to hobby craft sequences and bows and bits and bobs, lots of writing sticking we had to do to this to keep the costs down, because money was too tight to mention' thanks simply red for that quote.

So Michilas great skills on designing them did sure save us a pretty penny, or two, so we both came up with a master plan and how we could save even more money, we got our heads together and came up with a magical plan to save even more hard-earned cash. We decided to ask our friends and families to buy us wedding gifts but instead of conventional toasters and kettles and dining sets, which we had already we had all this because we had already set up our home and already purchased all these items. We asked our friends and families if they could, club together and say pay for the DJ to which my friends billy, Howard and Vicky and Ken and Jane, Ken being the match maker who got us together in Chicago's, they all chipped in that was the DJ sorted fantastic. We now have music, to which we decided to have music and karaoke also, but we didn't have all the guests singing and putting in requests because we didn't want it to turn out like a bad karaoke night with poor bad singers, so we selected people to sing, Ken sang, please release me let me go by Engelbart Humperdinck which we did question why the bloody hell would you want that at your wedding we all laughed, but I loved that song, because my dad sung it also and it had fond memories. I sang your just too good to be true this was by Andy Williams and it happened to be the song we first danced to, when we met on the night of 17th June 2006. The best man and best mate Jeremy sang let me entertain you' by Robbie Williams who was our favourite artist and also we sang together one song which was one of mine & Jeremys favourites, which was get on up by five, which we sang many times together at the local pubs, we do love a bit of karaoke. It's got to be said then a friend from our local sang forever in blue jeans by Neil diamond, I love my music which was my therapy many years previously. Lots of other people wanted to sing and asked to sing when they get a little inebriated and confident but we didn't want that we just selected these few, who we knew could sort of sing so it wasn't a typical bad night of singers, but the DJ did it in between the music of which he was playing so it broke it up very nicely indeed and wasn't a boring karaoke set.

So other things to pay for was the cake which a great expense which Michilas mum and dad kindly paid for thank pam and Fred.

My sister bought the book that everyone signs which was a lovely keepsake thank Samantha.

My wife and I paid for the church and the car, which we had a lovely white limousine. My mother paid for the food and my father put money behind the bar also which was a great help, thanks Mum and dad. Everyone went home with a full belly of beer and food. We got discount on the flowers which was a family friend of Michilas which gave us a massive discount, which decorated the church and the reception on all the ten tables which we had, everything looked absolutely fantastic and me and Michila put a considerable amount of money behind the bar which lasted till 11pm ish what was most of the evening considering. Considering we got married at 3pm and was back at the reception at 5pm ish, my sisters' boyfriend at the time offered his time and did all our photos because he loved photography and didn't charge us. My sister's friend and my friend did the video for nothing also so saved us a lot of great expense. So, everything was in place for the perfect day and everything to go without a hitch, excuse the pun.

So, onto the 25th June 2011 was time for the stag do, of which my best man Jeremy organised, it was very very well organised might I add, we all had t-shirts everyone who attended which was about 12 or so I believe. He had all our names printed on the t-shirts which was very funky. We first all met up at a race track, which was home of go carting, which most people got invited in. It came to the face and unfortunately I came 2nd place and Jeremy the best man won, but hey we had loads of fun and everyone had a good booze up afterwards which was good, but I remember the rhyme at school that everyone used to say was 1st he worst, 2nd the best, 3rd the one with the hairy chest, so on that I was the best.

Then we moved onto town, of which we all had pizza in town and then went on a little public house crawl, which everyone was getting rather merry at the time, so stag being stag it wouldn't be a stag if you didn't end up in a strip joint, oh dear we did, so town centre being such a well to do place, home of derby foes have believe it or not a strip joint, so we all went in there, which was let me say a very good one. Not that sort of think really floats my boat. God I am a good liar, ha-ha.

So, we were in there for a good 2 hours or so then we decided to go to a night club, which these days trades under the name of fever, which in my day when I first used to go there was Chicagos it changed names several times, in there we were enjoying good time, drinking dancing and have a bloody good time and we looked around and a couple of strippers from stir had obviously got dressed and come down and followed us into the night club to my amazement. They tried to coax us all back to the strip bar, one of my Mate was very tempted, they obviously wanted us to go back and spend our hard-earned money in their establishment of which we refused at first, I think a few of you may have gone back last knockings if my memory serves me right. So when the night was over we all left a little drunk, I walked home with My Mate and my Dad and I remember ringing my wife to be, just past the old west park hospital ground, to give us a life the last bit of the way of which she came out and did bless her, love her, she did everything for me, love her because we were tied and drunk.

And I remember my best man Jeremy leaving a little earlier than the majority of us, it came out after that night, that his youngest child was conceived that night, so a lot of good came out of that night also, love ya Jeremy and Family.

So that's the stag do done and dusted. Onto the big day, 2nd July it was here before you could say Jack Robinson. So, we were all excited I had stayed at Jeremys the night before the wedding for obvious reasons not being able to see the bride the day before the wedding. We played fifa 2010 and Jeremy beat me something like 16-1 at football on the game console. The play station was a good use that eve, we were listening to music and drank a little and just chilled, well I tried to. I was very nervous had lost a lot of weight leading up to the big day, I always lost weight when I was nervous, but Jeremy did a fantastic job, keeping me calm and getting through this big occasion in my life. I was so worried that the pressure of my wedding was going to take its toll too much on me and my bipolar was going to rear its ugly head once more. So, the morning of the wedding came fast, Michila being Michila who was to make sure everything was ok, had to drop of something to the venue of the reception which was kings meadow and she likes to check everything was set up ok, tables etc. for the big reception. But when she arrived there to her astonishment there was nothing set up at all the way I am or so. She was told the chairs and tables were not enough for our wedding because they were being used for another venue, in the next room or something, so nothing was set up at all to how we had originally arranged with the organisers, oh no disaster was striking again. So lucky I was friends with the secretary of the club at the time, was Vicky and luckily, she knew the chairman of the football clubs phone number., So Michila got straight on to Vicky. In the meantime, who gets wind of all these shenanigans, yes you guessed it me. So me as you could imagine was pacing up and down Jeremys flat, Oh my god, panic was an understatement the nerves built and built, but I was lucky to have my best man there to calm me down and said it will get sorted, my reply at the time was1 I have 150 guests coming and no bloody venue for them to come to'. So, meanwhile I get a phone call from the wife to be, calm down Darren I am getting it all sorted. So meanwhile she was calling Vicky, who then called the chairman who explained I was an Avid afc Wimbledon supporter of which the chairman sent some more people down to sort all as well as Michila had to get ready for the biggest day of her life (besides the birth of our daughter, so Vicky was down there organising everyone and getting the venue perfect, Vicky love you for all your hard work and Howard without you we wouldn't of had a reception at all. It's a good job Michila had to drop something off to check everything, I believe everything happens for a reason. Someone was looking down on us that day that's for sure! Thanks everyone involved we did get a couple of bottles of champagne out of the club for the cock ups and more of a discount because as you can imagine we did have a little complain because of the stress etc. which caused on the day of our wedding, so it all got sorted.

On to the pre-wedding drinks, we all arrived, well not everyone a few uncles and aunts and Vicky and Howard about 1pm ish or so for a couple of pints to settle the nerves. We all heard about the goings on that Vicky, bless her had to deal with earlier in the day. So, a few drinks we said, But Jeremy said 2 pints is enough mate, you don't want to be slurring your vowels at the wedding, so I listened to the advice of my mate, my rock and did what I was jolly well told.

So, 2.20pm came so we were dropped up the church in case of any early arrivals, so we could greet them of which my friend with the video was coming and previously he had been to the house where Michila and her bridesmaids and sister were there also. Our Bridesmaids were our daughter, her niece, Jeremys daughter, my niece was bridesmaids also and my nephew and Michilas Nephews were all page boys, so it was quiet a procession going down the aisle. So, we were all waiting for the guests all to arrive at the church. My aunt and my Uncle were early I recall and my 2nd cousin, my auntie bless her was a bit confused and called me Bob, thinking I was my dad cause I did sound and look like him. But later, we found out she has now been diagnosed with Alzheimer's, so that was the early stages setting in.

So, everyone started to arrive. We were then told to go in the church because 3 o'clock was about to arrive. She had already drove past early, when everyone was still outside the church and was shoed away to do another circuit around the block, St Marys Church top of the Avenue was the church of which I lived previously down the road and grew up going to this particular church as a child going to Sunday school also there as a young lad.

So, the bride arrived started to walk down the aisle, it was a lovely sunny day and quiet warm I recall. When Michila started to walk down the aisle, the nerves really kicked in, my 2 pints came out of me like nobody's business, in sweat. I mean all down my back my back was socked through, damb I knew I shouldn't have had though drinks. So, the beautiful bride arrived (oh I forgot thanks Sister in Law for lending Michila her wedding dress it fitted like a glove). The service went like a dream, I have a small thing I am a bit particular about that I hated wearing, black socks I only wore white sweat socks, I never wore dark socks I hated them like a venom, I still do to this day. So the service and the vowels were read and it came to when we were blessed and I knelt down and what was showing, yeah you guessed it my white socks, Vicky my friend had noticed this and took a lovely photo of this which was I recall I think put on that lovely social media page that most of us used as 'Facebook' thanks Vicky ha-ha lovely memory to look back on.

So the service was coming to an end, we walked down the church aisle, all leaving and our friend from the leather bottle pub who we drank with on out Friday night karaoke nights, put a pair of these wobbly glasses on to which we all cracked up laughing, but it did what he set out to do, it got the most perfect picture of use smiling naturally, which we still have up on our wall now, which is a perfect picture. Thanks Mate. Cracking idea.

Then it was time for the photo which took a good hour or so seemed to go on forever because to be honest all I wanted was a pint or Kronenberg which kings meadow served at the time, hence us picking that venue because Kronenberg has been my favourite tipple for as long as I can remember, probably from the age of like 16/17. So, we arrived at the reception everything was great we all sat down for the reception, to which was the best bit in my eyes.

Now we all needed a drink after all this waiting around taking all those photos. The speeches were so funny Jeremy you're a star. Let's make a toast he said and he had a piece of toast with him, so my dummy of a speech I played some AFC Wimbledon music, then I mentioned everyone who was at the venue, Like Angie and Les who were from Bognor or nearby there and I said oh we beat them at Football because AFC Wimbledon had played them. Then I said we have my Uncle and Auntie from near Mansfield oh we beat them at football, we had family from Tooting and oh of course you guessed it we had beaten tooting and Mitcham Football club at football also. I have been following and supporting AFC Wimbledon for as long while since we got started from all the MK split, which we don't like to talk about but we know who the real dons are AFC Wimbledon, new journey began after the split in 2001 with Wimbledon FC being sold and our football league status position in the league being stolen by M K. Who was to blame the FA of cause for letting all happen in my option, but this is a debate that can go on for many hours in pubs etc., all over the place I have people still approaching me saying oh do you go to M K to watch your football club and now after all these years just can't be bothered to explain that whole history thing after 17 years I just laugh off and say yeah good one, but we are now playing our football in league 1 of the English football league and the other lot which we tend to call franchise not MK, play in league 2, so who had the last laugh, yes we did, that enough about football, back to the wedding.

Everything went off brilliantly, it was a day to remember and I loved every minute of the day, but it went so fast you have to saviour every moment because you always get that person before you marry who says enjoy every moment and you think to yourself yeah yeah but they are so right. You turn around and that day is over because you feel you are on show, everyone wants a piece of you to look at you and the time to say congratulations, you feel like a celebrity that's for sure.

After the wedding and everyone had a good drink (on us I had guests, family members also coming to me saying what a wonderful wedding, take this money as this is what I so would have spent on drinks /beverages. You have this cash thanks it was such a lovely wedding, so I think Michils and I did pretty fine job in preparing it all and getting it all put together, well it was all down to the wife.

Me very surprised I had stayed out of hospital and didn't go down the mental health route after losing all the weight and the stress of the wedding getting everything prepared, didn't take its toll on me that for sure, but a good woman is all I need at this time to keep me out of what I nick named the big house of the mental hospital of lilac ward.

Thanks to everyone who attended the wedding it was simply the best thank you Tina Turner I will take that song quote because it may seem crazy, that music did keep my feet on the ground and was my therapy, to block out everyone and just be in my world and shut out everyone else to it and for us on getting myself well and back to life back to reality, thanks Soul II Soul I will take that song quote as well.

It's weird in my mind when I say something that is a song, I either think of it myself or start singing that gets me through tough and trying days, so the days are obviously harder to get over and through than others. Which music is my therapy it works all you bipolar people out there who are reading this book, don't take my word for it just do it and try it.

So, onto the honeymoon we decided to go to centre Parcs with my best friend Jeremy and Charlotte and their 2 daughters oh and their baby who was inside charlottes belly, thanks to the stag night. So, we arrived early

July out of term of course, so we got a much cheaper deal on our holiday, which was really half of the price, in the school holidays.

We got this fantastic house/villa and it had a hot tub (Jacuzzi) steam room, and also a sauna all the mod cons for a snip of the process, god I love a bargain. So, we threw all the luggage into the back of the truck, so much space because boy do you have to travel with so much stiff, when you had a 9-month baby. It would be easier if you could just take your house, the thing you have to take from high chairs to buggies, travel cots you name it we took it, besides the kitchen sink of course. We had so much fun on our lovely holiday with our best friends, I know it sounds odd hanging with another family, but we got on so well, it had to be done, Jeremy is my right-hand man, like my wingman to quote a film My Kenicke to me being Danny of course, ha-ha from the film Grease. My favourite film is Grease when you're feeling down, put it on it will put a smile on your face, sets up for your next Journey in the future to the Michael J fox films before me, the oldies really cheer me up, teen wolf, back to the future all of them. I love a film the old greats to lift your spirits when things are not cooking in your kitchen if you know what I mean.

So, we have 2 young children with us a 9-month-old and my mate had his 15-month-old with him, so you can imagine we had our hands full, oh and not to forget his oldest daughter who was 5 at the time, we have some great memories of that honeymoon. That will never leave, animals coming to your villa in the morning to greet you and say hi, deer's, rabbits, pheasants, it was like something out of Dr Doolittle, another cracking film, Mr Eddie Murphy.

So, the 2 weeks went with a bang really quickly as nearly as quick as the wedding day, but not quiet. We made the long drive home to continue with the rest of the year.

This year also we planned to have a loft conversion on my parent's bungalow, which got started in the august of this year. We wanted 3 bedrooms upstairs to give us more room to spread our things because we only lived on 1 level, currently, so it all began, builders again oh no thought

I was worried about the last time builders entered our home, I was ill, with the bipolar thing. So was it all going to happen again, history repeating itself. All the dust and dirt and rubble everywhere. But no I had Michila who is my mental saviour to keep me stable in my hour of need at this time, so she said don't worry it will be done soon,' we will laugh about all this when it's completed, but anyone can tell a bipolar sufferer to not worry its very similar, telling an alcoholic not to drink or a drug addict not to take the demon drugs!. So onwards and upwards the work began of converting our loft into a three-bedroom abode. Our 2-storey building for my family to live.

So, the completion was near very near we loved it. The beauty in building your own place is you have the chance to pick all your own home furnishings, colours and your own taste and your own mark on the place as it were. Of which we did, and it turned out pretty good, we did get ourselves into quite a bit of debt to get this underway, so that was a real worry too. Unfortunately, a lot of debt came our way, so there was only one way to get out of this mess and I decided to sell my beloved truck. My pride and joy my 2nd love of my life, my first being my wife of course. So, I said it, to release equity, to become more comfortable, moneywise and be able to breathe again, you know like the weight we have all been there, when you had a new-born, the expense is infinity and beyond thanks buzz light year for the quote. So, we did this got a cheaper car and paid for outright rather than having the dreaded monthly repayments coming out every bloody month. So, got a BMW 5 series years older but nice, it suited our needs at the time! Not as much room in the boot for our baby kit, but we managed it was a case of having to needs must and all that, it's all about cutting your cloth to the size of your table, I love that quote, one of mum favourites, thanks Mum.

So, Christmas came our daughters 2nd Christmas as our little family and went with a bang, New Year's Eve was good also celebrations were fantastic so now we are in 2012.

Still working very hard at Sainsburys, I became an online delivery driver now on the road delivering online groceries house to house, it reminded me of the day of my own business a slightly different as the orders were all made up for me, rather than me having to serve it all up and weigh it all on my scales the old fashioned way. I enjoyed very much delivering but it was very hard on the back, lifting because people always ordered heavy items, of course to save them carrying it from the supermarket. Which we all do. The whole point behind the service we all love to use. I did this for about a year come out of the store. It was very different to what I was used to, I was very alone out there because you were working solely on your town, which gave me a lot of waiting time, for customers to come home from work if you got early in doing your job efficiently, you had to wait for your time slots so people used to come home before these chosen slots, so waiting was boring and also I had to much thinking time which is never a great thing for a bipolar sufferer. Mulling things over and over in your head is never a great thing to do that for sure.

So, after the aches and pains and a few back and shoulder problems it was such a heavy job and took its toll on this nearly 40-year-old, who was starting to creek a bit on the old joints. Having time off when these injuries didn't please work that was for sure. But it was the occupational hazard of lumping and lifting all my chosen career in the joys of retail and being a strapping lad people just expected this of you because I was built like a tank and was weight lifting and attending the local gym on a regular basis. So was quilt built, my weight always has yoyo's up and down like tower bridge London, because of all the changes in medication all of my life, which was always an issue for me because it seemed like I was constantly on a bloody diet, which I hate and everyone does because we all love the food which aint good for us don't we, especially having a sweet tooth and being married and settled you get into your slightly comfortable zone and become putting on weight for fun because you're not on the clubbing no more you're not on show and you don't have to have that perfect body, really because you love that person whatever shape or size they become. You don't need image any more that what I meant you no trying to pick up woman as when I used to, only a memory now. Early nights and nappies were my clubbing now, going to bed when your baby goes to bed to catch up on those night feeds, which I may add I didn't do one because for obvious reasons my sleep pattern would have been all over the shop and that would have led to another possible mental hick up in my life. Which would have possibly led to another admission to the big house (i.e. hospital). So, thank you Michila for that favour, I did all day feeds and the last thing at night ones and let her have an early night on many occasions not that she needed her beauty sleep or anything, just to give her a better start to another challenging day of work and looking after a small bundle.

So that year was very normal if you can differentiate normal to a bipolar sufferer like me, we don't normally say are normally in the clouds high as a kite or we are in the hold of depression, which for me luckily I forget the lows only when medication make me that, Which are a different sort of groggy low, life for example for me if u drank coca cola or caffeine after 3pm I would not be sleeping at all that night that is what happens to me or I have had an evening out, chatting with friends at a party without alcohol, I would like hours to come back down to earth and switch my brain into standby mode, which I so wish I could at times of my life. I may unplug your brain and just switch off is a task so easy, for the majority of us, but for the minority of us 1 in 4 I think the statistics is for mental health suffers these days, it's not easy what so ever. So we were very lucky my Uncle Martin had a caravan, which was rented to us for a very cut price, being family thanks Uncle Martin & Auntie Angie, it did help financially was a great help when you are raising a family every penny helps, sorry that Tesco's ad, oh my god I am a dumb traitor, sorry Sainsburys it's only a quote ha-ha.

So, 2012 came and went pretty dam fast, it was quiet a good year by all accounts only bad thing was the sale of my beloved 4x4 truck oh well it's only a hunk of metal.

Ok so 2013 was here pretty quick it was going to be an interesting year because it was going to be my 40th year on this fine planet! Life beings at 40 some say, or its downhill from here who knows. I like to say naughty at 40, dirty at 30, nifty at 50. Funny how my weird brain works, so onwards and upwards. I live to tell another year to you fine readers. My birthday was looming March 20th so I was thinking what shall we do for it, go away with the family, do we arrange a big party (not really) even though I am a party animal and so love a good party, people that do know me would say I am a proper showman, or show off, I will let you choose on that. So, we just chatted about it, but didn't really arrange anything proper, just everything was in our heads, ideas but no real plans happening so March was here, bang wallop. So I always recall it happened something like this I went to a home game to watch the mighty AFC Wimbledon, my friend Colin who sat in front of us a very good mate, who I knew well it was funny I started talking to him when we first went to football at kings meadow Kingston that is not when we went to Selhurst park and plough lane, it worked out I said to him what your second name and he told me I got talking and he said he had a daughter I said oh ok, then he said what school she went to and I said oh I went there and it came about that I actually went to this same middle school with Julie, what a small world and we have been buddies ever since.

So back to the day, I get a text message from my mate, Colin. It read hi Mate shan't be at football today mate, I have a family friend get together to go to. So, I didn't think anything about it. He often texted me if he wasn't well or was on holidays, if he wasn't going to be at football, its juts a thing he did. So off I went to football as normal, dad took me to football as he always did that day. It was March 23rd we had played Morecombe at home, we had won 2-0 thank you Kevin saint-luce and Mr Jack Midson, so I was pretty damb happy. I noticed my friend Ken looked rather dressed up that day, so me being a bit of a dreamer being Pisces, sign of zodiac, I thought oh I know what the wife's done, she has arranged a surprise party after the game at kings meadow, so I thought what was going to happen was I would be asked to go to the back bar where we had our wedding reception and there would be a big surprise and there would be like 100 people to jump out on me. So, the game come to an end, final whistle went, we had won, which was a normal thing back in those days. So, I walked out of the ground thinking that someone was going to say Darren wait I wanna show you something in the back bar, but no it didn't happen to my dismay. So, we were driving back, dad and I which we always did on a football home game.

We got home my sister Samantha's car was in the drive way. I thought nothing of it, she always came and visited me and my parents, next door etc. So, I walked in my house opened the door to a massive surprise, surprise. My whole house was full of my friends and family, food all laid out, cake my wife had truly got me, I had no clue what so ever the surprise was a great one, well done Michila, that was a one up for that's for sure.

My bloody mate Colin missed the game to be there on my arrival home, bloody fantastic I said family gathering eh funny eh, he could have quite easily followed me home after the game and arrived at this surprise party after the big surprise thing, but he didn't, and I thought a lot of him for that, thanks Colin, thanks guys a banging surprise, I was absolutely flabbergasted to say the least.

The party went with a swing, good food fab company, Jeremy and family were there and a lot of my friends and family, good show Michila.

SO that was a damb go start at 2013, so spring had sprung and so had I, forty oh my god, where had those years bloody gone, I don't know, is the answer. So social media (i.e. Facebook) was full of my totally shocked face, thanks friends ha-ha!

So, 2013 eh! Was a very good year'

Sounds like the lyrics from a well know Robbie Williams song, talking of Robbie Williams, me and my mate Jeremy are massive Robbie Williams fans, I mean massive. So, we found out this year that Robbie was doing his tour and found out he was playing in Wembley, England. So, I had never been to see him live, I have always wanted to, Jeremy and I had often spoke of going to see him, but could never get tickets, because they sold out about 1 hour after going on release. So, Jeremy and I discussed maybe trying to get tickets this year to go and see 'the Greatest Showman' on earth in our opinion. Sorry stole the title from another film there. So, the big day came when the tickets went on sale, so all of us, me, my wife, Jeremy and his wife Charlotte were primed with the iPad, tablets, phones to get one step ahead of everyone else. Ticket master was the main site to get fastest access to tickets to see this great man. So, it was first thing in the morning I recall. So, on went the gadgets to try and be successful for tickets, so the take the crown stadium tour was imminent, fingers were crossed well everything was crossed. It was the time that the Samsung s4 phone came out so that will take you back. So, we all tried, me, my wife where having no luck getting through to obtain tickets. Then I got a phone call from Jezza aka Jeremy that was his nickname. You never guess what the phone call started, Mr Fry, he said because we always have called each other with Mr Fry and I Called him Mr Harris, just something we had always done, it's a London Thing ha-ha.

So, the conversation resumed, you never guess what I have only bagged 4 tickets for us all to go and watch Mr Robert Peter Williams in bloody concert, he might not have put his middle name in, Ha-ha and me I nearly fell of my chair, because we had all tried previous years and failed miserably. So, this was quite an achievement by Jeremy Harris, I must admit. So, we had them, fantastic it was June I believe we went, my 40th year, and it was around Jeremys birthday time which was June also. So, we all put our heads together, I think Jeremy suggested let's go to Wembley Stadium in style, so we only hired a fat white limousine, and all went up there in a stretched limo, we all felt like superstar pop stars for a day it was absolutely a great experience. I will never forget for as long as I live, we were quiet far away up in the gods of the stadium, but we sat and heard what was needed to give us that buzz that we all yearned for. So, we were all waiting with bated breath for the man to come out, but Robbie being Robbie that we all know didn't and doesn't do anything by halves. He came out of this massive bronze statue of himself and bloody zip wired out of his own mouth, which was bloody high up I can tell you. Absolutely fantastic everyone screaming and cheering. The atmosphere was electric to say the least, then the concert began, I must admit I did have a tear in my eye on many occasions, being there was so surreal because back in my earlier breakdowns Robbie was my saviour, in blocking out the world listening to his powerful lyrics he and guy chambers at the time had written such powerful ballads and songs. Thanks to them wonderful people I am still her today to tell the tale. So, the songs came rolling out the memories of hospital everything came pouring out of me the emotion was really powerful for me because of those reasons alone. He came out to 'Let me entertain you' which he had to really cause I telling you now he certainly did that.

But one of my all-time favourite songs and Jeremys also was 'Nans song' because it touched us in every way you can imagine because us losing our nans, please you take this song properly and listen, another of my favourite song are 'come undone' because that relates to me also, the trials and tribulations of my colourful life! Another song which I like is gotta be the classic 'Angels' which I have done karaoke more than a few times in my life. I do like 'Feel' the list is endless I could be here a while listing all my favs.

I will tell you about an experience I had back in 2004 when I had a blip of mental health, my mum bless her had found a lot of drugs that I had taken on previous breakdowns and I think they were probably out of date, I remember it well I was smoking cigarettes heavenly one after the other, like I did when I was ill and was standing in my mums back porch, sweating and not really my best, not eating, taking these concoctions of pills my mum said 'take these take this one you will be ok' bless her she was doing her best love her to death, so I took then only after realising they were like 4-5 years out of date. So, I carried on smoking didn't feel too great and suddenly I had this only I could describe it as a bad reaction of some sort. My parents were standing inside the bungalow where we used to live and suddenly my eyes were I though deceiving me I saw my parents in a different light, they had no skin on them, exactly like the video in Rock DJ by Robbie Williams. I don't know if it was a delusion of everything that had built up never experiences anything like this before. They literally looked like they were aliens from out of space, on my god, I thought I was going to die that day, think it may have been the lethal cocktail my mum bless her gave me by accident, not realising they were out of date. So that was an experience, I will never forget. That's for sure.

But it was as clear as the nose on our face, I started crying I remember that and came in sobbing and just hugged them both, it was certainly a very freaky experience, I like the swing stuff Robbie also did, Mr Bojangles, is great, Mack the knife I love and the great aint that a kick in the head the list is endless.

The other songs that are great 'me and my monkey' if you get a chance to listen to them, you will be inspired I feel that's enough of Robbie Williams, I thank you for the memories Robbie.

Just one more song quote 'lazy days is a cracking song. 'Old before I die' this earlier stuff inspired me also, sorry blabbing on about him, but remember music is and will always be my saviour.

Thank you 2013 that will be all for now

2014 Now was a very good year or very very good year. We decided me and the trouble and strike (wife) bit of cockney slang there ha-ha, to have another baby. So, January came after we had begun trying for another your one and Michila was late, no not or work, her bloody period excuse the pun. Didn't me to say it like that whoops! She was a week late or something, which sometimes was normal with her funny cycles 'Women eh' so we thought we would go down to our favourite all night chemist. The only chemist that never shuts, you know the one on the corner! So, we went in and bought the little gadget that you have to pee on. Just to see what was happening and bang yes on my god she was pregnant, yeah, elation and happiness hit me, and I was so happy I think we both had a tear and hug, which was a perfect moment that's Martine McCutchen, I will take that song quote, lovely. So, the scene if you imagine it, in the bathroom was absolutely a one for the old memory bank.

Ok so I worked on the fresh department at Sainsburys at this time, worked with a fantastic team at this time, my team leader at this time this year was good, very good in fact. What happened to come was not though, I was working as normal bringing in the pennies (Penny lover what a song) Sorry, quotes again. Anyway we were going out clubbing, during these days working with the great team, so we all decided to go clubbing for someones sort of occasions, there was an excuse., really to go out with the work lot bearing in mind, these people I was with were like 20 odd years my younger, but hey these lovely people invited the old boy out, me! We used to go around a colleagues house for pre-drinks which we did this particular night think it was like around April time. So, set the scene we were all round there sitting in his front room, his mum was there. Drinking also we were about the same age as I remember, joking with his mum saying my god you could be my son then, because what I was like back in the day who knew ha-ha., love you mate. So, we carried on drinking like you do ready to go, to the night club, afterwards. So, which we all did, my clubbing days were, kinda of over but I love dancing and expressing myself and letting it all out, emotions but doing karaoke as well, it was a massive release for me emotionally as well. Took the edge off everything when I was in my high time, episodes of manic, delusional behaviour, so drinking madly we were, like you do. So, you don't have to pay mad prices in these club, just buy a couple when you get in there. We all do it. So, Adam I mean was really getting it down him, always had an eye for the girls He'd, asking them out all the time and sometime getting knock backs, so like me it was untrue. He reminded me of me, when I was his age going through all my pain, 16-18 year old for me. Sorry getting side tracked again. Anyway, this particular Saturday night, we were drinking Jack Daniels, which was his tipple, he downed a hell of a lot, Adam was like me at that age kept things to himself. Chatted was a team player and a strong part of our team our team fresh. Which was our dept. So, we were all drinking smoking, getting mad, drink does funny things to you, as you all know, make you drink, sorry bad Joke. It takes you on your happiness journey, but is only a quick fix, temporary you come back down, those dark low places someone where thankfully I never go, so my bipolar is type 1, I get the awful highs, spending money, lots of it on small things not expensive things who knows, sorry getting bad to be in question. I thought to myself he is proper heavy on the booze, we all chatted having a cracking evening.

So off to the club we went, all in our cheap ubers like you do. Probably celebration AFC Wimbledon victory. Had a great night in the cheese room, 80's room love it in there, our 80s is all coming back its doing a turnaround, the music scene is always coming around again the 80's I mean, great night end of, hangover what a movie by the way. Like us really but without the drugs, well for me anyway never tried, only prescription stuff. Couldn't with my head, so good night had by all, so few weeks later I think it was Adam was admitted to hospital, same place as I was, back in the day, Elgar ward, I think not sure. He was more the other guys friend because I was older, I was like there great uncle, really big bear of wisdom to help them have a laugh, and a laugh we certainly did have. So back to work on the Monday, feeling good sort of hangover probably lingering, it did take days now were getting older. Take longer to bloody recover I can tell ya. So, it was going around on the rumour tree that Adam was in there, I thought no. It was like having a flash back of me.

So, he was in a couple of weeks I think or so and one morning bang. We had all got in to find out that Adam had died, can't remember who told me. Oh, the grief was awful losing a part of a team and a mate of course.

He came to light that he had slipped out of one of those, little windows that open outwards at the bottom at 45 degrees, you know the ones. Found him being so thin and then he climbed on the concrete chimney, in the grounds of hospital and we don't know, he may over be medicated high or drowsy on drugs been there for them battles and go right up to this say 60ft high chimney and was trying to be talked down by a security guard, I think. But unfortunately, sadly very sadly he lost his balance and came down to his death. RIP Mate.

So, the funeral was here, oh my god the grief was awful, god knows what his parents and family were going through. So, we all went to the funeral all the gang from work, the fresh crew. I called us the dough fresh (sorry music), google it. What pop band. We all stood there, my mate, my good friend my produce manager who gave me my break and gave me the job at Sainsburys, started me on my retail journey, thanks Mate.

Very sad, we were all leaving the funeral I said. Oh no I stopped in my tracks, Adams Mum, was there, I didn't know whose mum was working with him. Lads don't discuss them mums at work. So, leaving there she put her arms around me, I knew her she was my nurse when I was in hospital, long blonde hair, down to her bum. Lovely Lady. Looked after me on my admission in 1991. OMG what a small world. So, we had this big hug and cried. She said this would have never happened if it was when you were in Darren, you were upstairs in the wards, they changed it he was downstairs.

This is what happens when you don't open up and talk about your problems, please do it!

It was all taken to court a couple of years later, to ask why he wasn't cared for or watched properly. They won the day, got what they were looking for, got on the news on TV got the publicity its so needed.

Well done to his family for this. It should never have happened, the health services admitted negligence. Bill Withers 'a lovely day' come to mind. I was signed off after this for 2-3 weeks had a mental wobble and wasn't good at all. Then not long after this was the passing of another chap Graham (RIP Graham) who left behind my work wife from an accident in the bath from a seizure, so our place has had its fair share of grief and sadness, RIP Mate!

So 2014 was a fabulous start, another little Fry will be imminent, so we went for all the scans etc., we decided to find out the sex of the baby, but I didn't want to know at first, I wanted it to be a surprise at the day of the birth, love a surprise, used to cheer me up a lot. but Michila i was dead against it because women had to do all the planning like the bedroom, colours the decorations, the bloody colour co-ordinations, so we had a little deal that I decided we would both find out the sex and we wouldn't tell no one else, mum or dad on both sides or no one, which we shook on, so going through the pregnancy all out friends and family were all trying to find out trying to trip us up to find out what we were having well a baby of course' was my reply but that was the joke anyways. So, we went through the pregnancy me wrapping the wife in cotton wool making her eat loads of fruit every day, like a good husband should of course, to keep her and the new baby healthy. So, everyone was trying to find out, they all knew we knew the sex but to no avail everyone got nought out of us.

Jeremy thought we were having a boy, friends and family had their little theories, but no one was getting any info, this case was closed. Till the date arrived, when this baby was going to show its face.

I Can now reveal that 2014 was a mental year, but luckily again my wife kept a lid on the bipolar battle, no mental health issues, which was all good, you know what they say behind every man is a greater woman or something like that. She kept me calm and my feet firmly nailed to the ground, the love of a good woman, can save me, from fighting with myself mentally every day, which we all have these battles don't we. Because we were blessed with that lovely condition bi bloody polar! So, we had a long year this year 9 Months seems like an eternity, one of Robbie's songs which I love sorry no more Robbie song quotes I can't promise though ha-ha. But we were patient I was a very patient patient, even in my hour of need in the big house (hospital).

So lucky there was no admissions this year, it was going really well, this year. So our older daughter was an October baby and this new baby was due, yeah you guessed it October too, think that baby was due, like back end of October. So, we all are waiting, so October came we was all watching England v San Marino on the TV the family I mean well me and Michila and suddenly Michila was getting those twinges, I thought to myself come on don't be silly, not before the game ends, sorry only joking. So, they were getting slightly worse and worse as the enemy panned out. So, I said are they contractions, she said I am thinking it may be the start, it got to 9ish – 9.45 the game was coming to an end. England won 5-0, so good job thanks to Jagielka min 25, W Rooney min 43 penalty, Danny Welbeck Townsend min 72 and our goal to finish the game in minute 78, just if you were wondering who scored them, which you were probably not. So Michila decided to call the hospital to let them know she thought things were starting as it were. So, the hospital said the normal things how long are the contractions, they were quite far apart at the time if I remember rightly. So, they said hey just got to bed and get some sleep, you will need the energy later. So, we did exactly that. I dropped off quite quick, which was very rare for me because switching off was not easy for me at all. So, during the night I get a great big dig in the ribs, oh my god the wife says, I think we better go 2.30-3am it was if my memory serves me right. So, I got up like a shot out of a gun, and panic mode set in, where's the bag, are you ok, oh bloody hell.

I think the words came out. So, dad says he would take me I was a mess not really fit to drive to hospital. So, dad got woke while I was running around the house panicking, like we do fellas. So 3am in the car, foot to the metal ass, well not quiet in his Suzuki swift, ha-ha. We arrived at 3.15 suppose it was got in at the front desk, all the questions are being asked the normal rig moral, and michila screamed out soon as we arrived and then again like 2 minutes later, the nurse said I think you better go in, to which we did, we didn't even have time to book in properly. So straight into the birthing suite, blimey, I had only been awake like 40 minutes, Michila said 1 need a poo was her exact words the nurse said, no u think you do, come on the bed quickly, so she did. She was made with lots of energy after that 5-hour power nap, give me that bloody gas and air. I remember giving her the gas mask, but hence it wasn't even bloody switched on. She said rub my bloody back then, then anger started rub it then, she said don't stroke me I was in trouble like most men, while your other half is in labour.

Thought that I was strong your wrong, thanks Robbie last quote. So, I was rubbing her back she had a lovely fatty knitted cardigan on, at this time because it was October and it was cold. Outside, inside a hospital it was 80 degrees in there, the sweat was pouring off me I felt I was in a sauna. Nerves were in tatters and my stomach was in a reef knot. So suddenly a couple of big pushes and bang, the baby was here, while Michila was on all fours on the bed may I add. The baby swallowed some fluid, mcconamum, it thinks it was call and my god this baby was in a hurry to arrive into this big bad world.

So out the baby came and was handed into Michilas arms very quickly. The sex was another girl we knew anyway we kept ya all guessing, ha-ha. So, we were over the moon had no time for pacing up and down the corridors of the hospital drinking hot chocolate this time around that's for sure., This little lady was not hanging around. So that was that Michila had to stay in hospital for a couple of days because she had thyroid problems, from before and they wanted to keep an eye on the baby because of the swallowing of this fluid.

So the day of the birth was successful in every way, it was the time of letting everyone know, my mum I think I called first at 4.02am @Mum the baby is born she said blimey that's was quick you are joking, I said no, she said what was it I said a baby thanks Del Trotter from only fools and horses for that gag. No, I said really, it's another girl then I phoned Michilas mum Pam, she was over the moon too the whole family were, it was a perfect moment. So both of my girls were born on a Sunday which was nice, the only bad thing is they were born one week apart 10th October and 17th October, well something it's a good thing because we always have on big traditional party every year invite friends and family, and have one party for the 2 of them, kills 2 birds with one stone kind of thing. Which costs less in the long run, I suppose.

So, 2014 finished perfectly we now had a new born and a week away from a 4-year-old. So, it was a challenging time for all concerned. Previously this year 2014 in the summery, Jeremey and I had got the bug to the whole concert thing, so he decided to get tickets again to see Mr Robbie Williams again this time in a very smaller venue more compact the o2, so for him and his wife to go, which they got, but something happened and charlotte his wife couldn't make it, so she asked me very kindly if I would like to go and I snapped her hand off with no problem at all. So the o2 here we come, we decided to go about 5-6 hours before the concert started to get a very good standing position, we arrived at the o2 I think about lunch time for an evening concert, when we arrived the people were queuing with tents, chairs and has been sitting there a lot longer and we were amazed at how many people who were already there, we thought we were going to be in the front to the queue, but no we were very wrong do what we want that far from it, to be quiet honest maybe 200-300 people in front of us. So, we were thinking no bad position when we get into the arena. So, we were waiting and waiting, sitting, standing, eating, drinking, coz we didn't want to lose our place in the queue of course. So we were queuing like you do, got talking to a couple of girls in front who looked like they were regular concert goers, what gave it away they had like 2 batteries with them for their mobile phones and were talking about previous Robbie concerts they had been too, only one of them was on MK dons fan or what us Wimbledon fans like to call then franchise or MK Scum.

She saw my tattoo, which I have on my left arm of AFC Wimbledon badge and writing with AFC Wimbledon on it and the conversation and the arrangements and the whole history behind it all was dragged up, it was quiet fresh then, because the transition happened in 2001, well thirteen years ago of hurts as far as I was concerned.

So that went on for a bit well a lot in the end I just ignored her. So, we queued and queued, it seemed like days we had been there, so 6.30- 7pm came I think it was, and the big moment came, the doors being opened everyone cheered and cheered in the queue like you would never believe. So it opened the people started pouring in they opened like 6-7 different ones, which really made us look like we were further to the front of the arena, it was like the stage at the front and then there was like a catwalk runway coming away from the stage into a bit of a circle, so we got quiet close to the runway but there was like five or six rows of people in front of us, which wasn't too bad at all, result we thought.

So, it was time for the man himself to come out, we were much closer that last year at Wembley, which was cool. So, Robbie came out the stage seemed like ½ football pitch away from where we were standing, but we were right on top of the runway bit, so when he came out, he started his songs, remember him doing me and my monkey with monkey masks on which was hilarious. So, during his other songs a little way through the concert, he started to walk around the concert, he started to walk around the runway bit, when Robbie done this, we were only like 3 meters away from the greatest showman in our options of the world, which was pretty good to say the least. He was sweating and shaking his head and dancing, I think we got sweat dripped on us we were that close like. This other couple of girls we got talking to, said if me and my mate Jeremy are you two together, yeah we said we came here together, she said no are you a couple, we said hell no, best mate an easy mistake to make not we were mortified, so I said no we are married but to ladies not each other, so funny we can laugh about it now, but certainly not at the time. But great moments and a good time we had that's for sure. So the end of the concert was here time to bundle out that's what, it felt like the cow hoarding season or sheep dog trials, rounding us all up to get the train home, I can remember sitting on the train, Jeremy and I were not spring chickens and me 41 and Jeremy 38 at the time, our knees were shot sitting on the train for all those hours standing and the few hours watching the concert also, we had a good crack up and laugh about it on the way home, we could feel our knees they were numb as fuck excuse the language but no other word describe it really.

2015 was here now with a big bang before we could say Jack Robinson

We now have to fantastic daughters and life was quiet challenging to say the least and I coped mentally well that was the burning question. So for sure that I asked myself every single day, but again my wife was on hand to keep me on the straight and narrow a good wife is all you need, great family and great friends, I say thank you to every dame one of you because deep down I had always wanted children, but never thought it would happen to me because of that sigma, if you want to call it a stigma, of bipolar because it's not a very social conditions, its rather unsocial because of the bad things we all do us sufferers, like mood swings, stressing about everything, obsessing about everything, weight going up and down with meds, it's a long battle, fighting with all these contributes of the conditions us sufferers call bipolar. It's really hard pleasing everyone, just trying to be normal. I love the normal, does anyone know what is normal? How should we act who is your typical stereotypical normal person? Love to meet that person and shake their hand and have a jolly good chat with them to find out how we are supposed to behave and act and conduct ourselves, cos I just don't know do you?

So, 2015 let's get back to it, I went on a bit of a tangent then, a mad erratic rage, which we can so bipolar!

So this year was a good year also we had 2 children like I said beautiful girls and we were nearly out of space also, where we have our extension built by a friend of the family, he done a tremendous job, but with the top being on there we had built the loft conversion with very little head space and you could hardly get into one room with the slanting roof, so it was very practical at the time we got the top put on, we have run well over our project, in 2011, so we would of liked to have made it bigger at the time, but the purse strings wouldn't let us unfortunately. So we decided this year to put a dormer window in to square off the roof and give us much a bigger room, to which we did, first in our oldest's room, we pushed the dormer window out, which made her room like 3 times the size, which was fantastic because girls have got so much stuff, though I had a lot of stuff, but hell no girls have got so much more! So, then our youngest's room was a bit small also as we decided to push her side wall out which was slanting, also give us minimal space, so we did, we had some great builders who have carried out all our work in the past! At the time of this I was still at Sainsburys working away, I had moved back to the shop floor, away for delivery, because the old joints were creaking with all the heavy lifting, I had to endure. So, worked with a lovely couple of brothers. One working on the produce section and his younger brother working on Counters, but the younger one never much liked on and there and wanted to better myself. Cam had been very good at doing odd jobs for me around my place i.e. building decking, he was a great craftsman's and a damn good worker. So whilst our builder was working around my house, ripping roofs off, making dirty great holes in my roof and getting on with the job, Cam came around to visit me like he often did with his lovely girlfriend, she didn't come on this occasion, we were sitting there In the garden watching the lads crack on with the work and I suddenly said to the big boss of his building company.

Hey 'g' we called him, do you need any more help off another bloke on your firm to help you mate, he replied 'why' I said Cam here which is his nick name I used, very good and doing tiling and a great craftsman. G then replied right mate saying to cam, if your that good show me, cam having his best clothes on was not really dressed to carry out such tasks and graham said 'I need the plaster boards in that room up there'; 1st room I thought it was if I recall, putting up on the wall ready to be plastered, cam said ok, g was testing how good he really was, so cam went up there in his best clobber and grabbed an electric screw driver, within about an hour or so he had most of the plaster boards down and he came down and g said 'you serious you wanna job?' and cam said 'Yeah' G was a little impressed with his craftsmanship and said to him 'can you start Mon?' think it was a Friday the day in question. So, cam got a new job in the builder's trade where he belongs Love Ya Cam', he deserved a break got one and he has never looked back, don't know about G thought Ha-ha.

Cheers G for giving my mucker a break also.

So, a few weeks went by in the back of my head was also oh no bloody building work again it is gonna affect me mentally. With all the stress of the dust and the mess, coz I am OCD I do like everything in its place and a place for everything, Sorry Michila I drive her senseless, saying that to live there that mess, why did you leave that there she is also more laid back than me and leaves stuff occasionally around the house in odd places, I do get on her back, but my mum said even when I was a kid I was always a very tidy young man and always kept my bedroom really tidy and didn't like clutter, so I suppose its in bred in me as it were. So, I still worried that the old condition was gonna rear its ugly head again but luckily my wife said don't worry about it you cant change anything, it is what it is, and I hate that saying god it gets me very vexed, but I suppose she is right. I never really admit that a woman is right that often, ha-ha. So, the work was coming to an end it was actually finished, it looked fantastic, Cam for his input also, looks splendid to say the least. So, everyone was happy, our youngest why hell she was too young to appreciate it all only being just near 1 years old!

So it was time to get everything straight which didn't take long because Michila and I do make a fantastic team, when we have a job or two to complete I think that has kept us cemented together after the years, I think to myself, it must be so hard for her, living with bipolar also, god she needs a medal being married to me, one as big as a 'soup plate'. One of my Dad's sayings, thanks Dad for that, I will have that one! So, we go to Cam to get our tiling in the bathroom, which he did a fantastic job, what a tiler and then he put our Italian floor tiles down in the kitchen/diner area which he did a sublime job, mates' rates of course. So, 2015 was a trouble-free year in terms of illnesses of the mental health capacity I mean.

So far so good I had been clean as it were for seven good years, bearing in mind my cycles are normally every century, that ten years cause is the 1989,1991 and the 1999, 2001 so I wasn't really due for one until 2018, oh no can't wait for that year folks. Fingers crossed the wife can keep me on the straight and narrow once more for a long time to come, Love You Michila. It is killing me worrying when another admission of delusion or episode is gonna happen I am always worrying when the next one is imminent, born bloody worrying just like my nan was she was always worrying love her. When I used to go anywhere like scout camps when I was a young whipper snapper. God bless your soul nan miss ya, love ya, would love to have an a phone conversation with her once a month, just to put the world to rights, but that's not an option, getting a bit emotional right now, must stop and snap out of it. Right I am cool now and relax breathe.

AfC Wimbledon still doing ok, holding our own in the league, I renew my season ticket along with my dad every year, I love my football and my car two of my failing if you like, but we all have a cross to bear don't we there.

So swiftly onto 2016 it was gonna be a good year, my wife's 40th year, so I had been planning her birthday for quite a while during the bad ere of 2015, because it was quiet a big day to plan, I was going to arrange a surprise party, I do love to bring myself a lot of stress, which I shouldn't do bearing in mind what can happen? Mental! Oh well your only 40 once in your life, so I thought a massive surprise party with 100 guests will be challenging to do, when I was keeping it from the wife, my soul mate who keeps me cemented together, I was playing solo this time, no wing man. Well Jeremy was there to help me when I needed him. So, I started texting people the dated back in 2015 think I started doing it 6 months prior to her birthday, back in July or so 2015. So, the texts were going back and forwards like mad, I was getting from the wife 'who you texting' like they do. 'No one love' was my reply just the bloody work group, I blamed my manager at work he got the blame many times, my manager was always there for me also in my hour of need, somewhere to off load my problems and so the preparations were in full swing for this surprise 40th.

I was texting everyone every month to keep reminding them all, it was a really stressful time. I am telling you. February 2016 was the date I went and booked the venue which was gonna be the golf club, which was a lovely place, we have previously used for our youngest's christening one year prior to this occasion. Both the kids had been christened because our eldest went to St Mary's church of England school, we regular attended church in our old community which was St Marys and when we moved, we attended St Marys when we moved parish. our vicar there and you couldn't meet a better man, he is a lovely man, luckily where I work Sainsburys, our PR guru at Work donated every year to our Christingle, served oranges and mince pies which we are eternally grateful and we get vouchers and Easter eggs donated also for the school fairs of which we were heavily involved. We do a lot for charity the wife and I, raising money it's only so our kids can have a better start and future in their journey in life. So back to the 40th sorry went on a bit of a tangent there.

Just when something gets in my head, I have to get it out, it is also a very good thing for bipolar sufferers little tip that worked for me recently, is write everything down on paper or your mobile phone calendar, don't use your brain as a memory bank, because you always worry about what you have to do stuff or go somewhere then when you have carried out your tasks you can cross them off the list our delete it from your phone memory etc...

So, the venue was booked for this surprise party, food was sorted which they were gonna do at Horton it was just the hard bit I had to do and that was to pay for it, Mum lent me the money and I paid her back in instalments if I recall correctly. So, the DJ who used to be the guy who did the karaoke of which we attended regular on a Friday night down the leather bottle. He was a good DJ and was always very good after a party.

So that was arranged. Off the list. It was just getting everyone there at the right time and of course how I was gonna play it with the Mrs! So, I put the old thinking cap on to how I can do this? So I thought of a good idea I could tell her I am taking her away for the weekend to which I did tell her that is, so everyone was told to get there for 6.30 pm, the place is like 3 min drive from our place I might add, so, the day of the party was here oh no my nerves were shot to pieces is everyone gonna be there on time is she gonna see someone's car in the car park, oh my god. I did like putting pressure on myself which is shouldn't do in my current state of mind. So, I thought how can you throw another red herring in to the mix, the evening of the party was here. I got her in the car, with a blind fold on of course, coz I wanted it to be a surprise when we arrived at our destination. Which was a3 minute drive up the road, so I decided to take her round the M25 for 30 minutes or so just to think she was going somewhere further away. We had already put the kids to bed, I might add, and mum and dad were baby sitting next door which they had the baby alarm listening for the kids but no, when we left at 6.30 ish my mum and dad woke the kid to get them changed and at the party before we arrived. It was all planned it was like a military operation everyone knew their positions and the destination and where they had to be at a certain time. So odd we went for a ride around the motorway, still blindfolded of course. So, we then arrived around 7.30pm ish at the venue! Got her out of the car and she had not a clue where she was, she thought it was just a romantic weekend just the 2 of us, you can make it if you try just the two of us, you and I. Sorry about that just broke into song for no reason at all I do that sometimes at home, annoys the life out of the wife or that rhymes so I am at it again 'sorry seemed to be the hardest word' that Blue & Elton John for the one love that time, you tube it, go on right now on your mobile have a break from the reading take 5!

So up the steps was fun at the venue, with a blind fold on, health & safety at the highest degree, oh my god that was a hard thing to do let me tell you.

So up the stairs we went I had already texted Jeremy my main man to keep everyone quiet the 100 guest or so which he did.

So, we finally finished the journey up the stairs, so glad she hadn't had a pre birthday drinks, could have ended up at the bottom of the stairs with me on top of her, thank god we tackled the stairs, it was a weight lifted off my head we got to the top and opened the doors of the party room. We opened the doors and our youngest shouted being a year and a half old Mummy I was just about to take the blind fold off and michila Said was that our baby I took It off just and said yeah and everyone shouted surprise surprise and there you go the rest is history, thanks everyone who attended, Uncle Kevin from the coast, Uncle John, Auntie Pat from Kent, Uncle Martin and Auntie Angie, my Uncle our friends from football Vicky, Howard, Ken & Jane. Colin & Jenny, his daughter & her girls, my sister Samantha and her husband Mark and my niece and nephew, Michilas great Uncle, don't worry I'm not going through the whole guest list. I had you going there though didn't I, do love a good joke and get people going, ha-ha. Yeah it all went with a swing a good old fashioned family get together and knees up, sorry forgot all of Michilas, brother, wife & children and Michilas sister Alana and other sister Erika and her husband Michilas lovely niece and everyone else who came who I can't name everyone because it's getting a bit boring, sorry reader that bloody tangent of mine again, must be the you guessed it bipolar, obsessive compulsion disorder behaviour be gone with you, I say!

So, all was to do now was party like Russian thanks Robbie Williams for that pretty marvellous tune. Go on you tube dare you if you haven't heard it. Ok put your phone down and keep reading, ha-ha. So, the end was near, and we faced the final curtain' actually we did all sing to that as a massive group on the dance floor, think it was the last song of the evening that's Frank Sinatra, my way god bless your talent RIP.

So, we loaded up my car with all the lovely presents that all Michilas lovely guests and family and friends had bought her. Thank you everyone. Then we walked her rather inebriated, drunk to all your young ones who don't know the old-fashioned jargon! It was only a 10-minute walk I think it took us 30 minutes though, one step forward and three steps back, thanks Paula Abdul once again cracking lyrics, you tube it young ones you want to remember that one! So odd we went home a lovely drinking sleep, god

I slept well that night, belly full of beer and the stress lifted off me like a ten-ton weight around my neck had gone zip-a-dee-doo-dah, zip-a-dee-day, (gonna stop this) my oh my what a wonderful day plenty of sunshine plenty of rain zip-a-dee-doo-dah, zip-a-dee-day! Ah thank you I hear you all clapping into a frenzy! So quiet a start to the year that was 2016 I was 43 in the march not much else happened that year really only looking after 2 young nippers, ankle biters, dustbin lids (kid) cockney rhyming slang not that I am a cockney, but oh well onwards with 2016 looking after a nearly 6 year old and a nearly 2 year old was very eventful at times let me tell you. Always remember my sister in law saying to me once oh not two don't get fighting you have got girls and I have 3 boys I get it all the time and I just said you are joking aint you. I said you have them for a couple of hours and see, she laughed if you have kids you will definitely be on my wave length with this one!

We lost yet another mate Chris Williams who was under the mental health also, he unfortunately was at the train station and fell on the tracks, don't know what happened, bless him! RIP Chris and only he knows. His step dad Steve I knew he was a fisherman, mobile I used to pitch up with him, with my mobile shop, many many years ago. Probably they 2000 or before, small world again RIP Chris.

The funeral was awful as they are but a lovely send off to a lovely lad. Why didn't he come and chat to me or someone's we need to talk people, communication!!!

So onto 2017 we had another selsey holiday in the caravan thanks to Uncle Martin and Angie once again, the kids enjoy Bunn leisure so much the entertainment is sublime and there is so much to do from pantomimes, wrestling on a Wednesday of course, evening entertainment bunny club for the kids to go to keep them entertained, while the parent get drunk, well me I mean, Really! We went this year with Alana and Mick we spent a week together it was great we had some laughs and some very drunken moments thanks for our company, Mick and Alana you are both stars. We had a lot of enjoyment that week. Bingo which I might add Mick won, Mick decided that night to treat us to bingo cards and we changed tables that evening if I recall where we normally sit because I always used to queue early to get a good seat anyone who has been there will know what I am talking about. So, we all sat there played our bingo, which we did most nights and then suddenly Mick shouted house, bingo whatever it was won over one hundred pounds, which was fab then they carried on again like they do. I then suddenly shouted house and then I shouted OMG been coming for years and I have never won, and the bloke said 'you aint won nothing yet mate gotta check your numbers see if it is not a fake claim' anyway he checked it and yeah I had won over one hundred pound also, so we had a good night that night I can tell you that, treated the kids as we always do, bought them a Buster Bunny each, Mick and Alana did thank you so much you lovely people.

So, this year was a bit boring really, well my life is far from boring but not a lot happened I mean mentally of course. My family were growing up way to fast that was for sure, blink of an eye, it all changed they grow up fast blink and you miss it all, you parenting out there will know exactly what I am on about! Enjoy them when they are young everyone advised but that is the best advise you can be given cause it goes like 'Flash' oh ah saviour of the universe, what a kids programme 'Flash Gordon' when I was a kid being an 80's kid was fun growing up.

With the Atari console and all over those 80's gadgets, for which I wish I still had them today I would be worth a small fortune, evil kanevil, the thing you used to wind the handle and the motor bike when cycling off this red base unit, one of my favourite which was the big track basically this was a like bigish tractor toy which you programmed like a robot. 4 steps forward. 3 steps right, length back and it was massive in its day, I loved it. I had like a week or so for Christmas or birthday I think and then my sister, put it on and set it off whilst it was on the breakfast bar and it went on the floor with an almighty smash and that was the end of that the wheel snapped off, dad tried to fix it with super glue, think he got his fingers stuck together, more than fixing my favourite gadget toy, anyway thanks Samantha ha-ha not to sorry sister eh.

The thing about bipolar is that your memory is so good I can remember every detail as a kid what I did going back 40 old years which is quite remarkable, I know we all have memories of our childhood and things stick in your memory! But not conversations and stuff I can remember weird but true!

Ok here we are then the present date 2018. Well the century has gone by since the last episode of my bipolar and admission into hospital. So, our youngest started nursery bang, where has the time going, Our eldest still in year 2, enjoying her schooling the year has started very calm, indeed so far so good, it started like a gentle centre. January our youngest started her nursery, going really well and she loves it and has loads of lovely friends and a great teacher, who really is a great teacher. My oldest daughter had her too, which she enjoyed also being in Nursery.

Michilas birthday came 12th February, went out for dinner, nothing heavy duty she is only 42 and me 45. My birthday came went out for dinner to which was a very sombre affair, everything calm, going brilliantly, it was always in the back of my mind, ten years and the sequence of getting ill was kind of, not bugging me, but there wasn't worried just in the old memory bank. My nephews 18th of which we went around my sisters for a lovely BBQ, thanks Mark for doing all the lovely a la carte 'cooking on the stove'. 18 my god it seemed like only yesterday I was nursing him, to sleep and taking him later in life to the local park and then taking him to play footy.

And my favourite talented niece who is now a hairdresser working in a shop and getting wonderful training to be a hairdresser, she is training really well, well she's 21 this year also so quite an expensive year, An 18th, 21st niece and nephew and also Michilas niece is 18 at the end of the year, also my god a lot of big birthdays this year and my friends Charlottes 40th.

So, let's move onto May, May the 4th or may the 4th be with you thanks 'Star Wars' I will have that one, god I love my quotes!

It was Uncle Kevin's 60th, so my favourite band, ultra 90's who me and my family have seen 3 times before once at selsey & twice at Banstead park. Which they put on every year, we do like this band, they play all the massive 90's anthems, they are so good it's like stepping back in time, to when I was like 17-25 years old, so many great and bad memories were involved in that time of my life.

So back to Uncle Kevin's 60th. I was looking on the website of Ultra 90's tour dates and blimey saw that they were playing at Hastings, on May 4th, the day funny enough I gave up smoking, 1 year ago 2017, so it was the anniversary of that to tell a lie, I don't smoke regular any more, I just smoke when I go out and drink alcohol more of a social smoker these days. We hardly go out drinking only once in a blue moon, love that song Elvis Presley rendition of course, Blue Moon, I saw you standing alone. Without a dream in my heart, ok you tube, sorry had to do it. Music is my therapy remember and my saviour, sorry to keep harping on about it, but it's the truth, it gets me through it all. So round Michilas mums one day we were chatting as you do, I was saying I am booking up to go and see ultra 90's at the coast, they are playing at a Caravan park so we thought we could do it all in one go and have a bit of a do for Uncle Kevin's Big 60th. So, Erika & her husband were sitting there we were chilling watching soccer Saturday on sky watching the results, roll in like we did on a Saturday cos I never worked Saturdays for obvious reasons being a football day. Michila's family are all Chelsea fans, well we can't all be perfect, only joking people. Love you all.

So, chatting away I said to Daniel I had been looking at prices for caravans and their cheaper deal were on an 8-birth caravan, so I said to him 'Do you fancy coming along to experience this bank, who are absolutely fantastic, he said yeah why not. So, we booked it, job done. So that was us 4 my family and his lovely family of 3 of them, so that made 7 in an 8 birth plenty of room. Will be great we thought. So, all booked and then Fred and Pam, Michilas parents, said on we could stay at Kevin's for the weekend to and make a short break of it as it was a bank holiday also. So great they told Uncle Kevin that's what they were gonna do, watch this band and Uncle Kevin's birthday not being till the 12th, don't think he really connected the trip, with being connected with his birthday really. It was the band of Ultra 90's that we were really mainly going there for, but little did he know what was going to unfold. Michilas sister Alana said I will come for the day and come to but don't tell Uncle Kevin will be a surprise then, Michila phoned her 2 uncles Uncle Kevin's brother, Uncle John and Auntie Pat and Cousin Uncle Martin and Auntie Angie and they said oh sure we'll book up also and get a caravan for the 4 of them to share to which they did, being a bank holiday. This place was getting booked up pretty fast because they were some sort of football tournament going on also, so Michilas brother and his wife and their boys, said we will come down too, they tried to get a caravan, but they were all booked up unfortunately, so they stayed at Uncle Kevin's also. Uncle Kevin I may add knew nothing about everyone coming, we kept it all a secret to surprise him. He thought he was just gonna meet us while Ultra 90's were playing, Kelly & Chris front this wonderful bank. Who you can check out on at their website they do weddings, party events they are pretty damn awesome, I am becoming a bit of a groupie bit sad really, I know at my age, but music you guessed it is my therapy.

So we were getting quiet a group together now, Uncle David and Auntie Tina along came for the evening, also Uncle Kevin previously said to me on the phone they won't come it's not their scene, so I left it at that, but they did and his daughter, Michilas Cousin came also and boyfriend and their 2 beautiful girls. So, it was building and one of Kevin's friends also turned up, so he just thinks it Fred and pam and just us all in one caravan, me and my family and Erikas family.

So, the afternoon of Friday 4th May was here, we arrived, Uncle Kevin came to meet us when we all arrived for a pint or ten, because we all loved a beverage. I can picture it we were sitting in the bar the club house bit, chilling like you do with 2 kids running about, what happened, all the aunties and uncles arrived. That was his first surprise. Then the evening came, the band, were poised to come on around and house to go, then Uncle David, Auntie Tina arrived along with Michilas Cousin and their kids, the surprises were endless for Uncle Kevin to arrive, so we had let's just say a pretty good get together and a great celebration. Uncle Kevin stayed in the Uncles caravan all weekend as his house was being used by Michilas brother and family and then Fred & Pam arrived on the Saturday, coz they had to look after the dog.

So, by Saturday we had a full set of people, so back to the evening of the band in question, the band came on and I was waiting to see Kelly & Chris and co, but the other band are on because they have more than one set of singers in their little set up!

To tour the whole country would be pretty hard I suppose to do it all themselves, this young lady came on, with her musicians, she was good, it was different to what Kelly and Chris do, it was ok, but I was expecting Kelly and Chris who duo together also as a couple. This band did the wedding of Rylan Clark-Neal in 2015, the guy that did rather well on x factor, google him if you don't know him it will all come back to you. So I was a little disappointed this young lady was pretty good, but I must admit I do prefer Kelly on lead vocals, she has been doing it a lot longer, but we did drink and it turned out to be a very good night, it wasn't all about the band, it was to start with when the idea was fresh and then it became only a small part of it. It was all about celebrating Uncle Kevin's birthday, his 60th, He was very shocked bless him, so that was that. So, goggle them Ultra 90's tribute band, check them out go and see them you won't be disappointed we certainly are not when we saw them!

So that May pretty done. An expensive year with an 18th, 21st 60th already gone and we haven't hit June yet, only half the year gone.

The summer was here and oh my god we had 2 months of that massive heatwave at 90 to 100 degrees, thank god for my air conditioning I had installed in my loft conversion it was a god send I can tell you. My room was dropped from 86 degrees to 65 degrees thank god for that.

So this year was battling on like bad test match at lords, hate cricket, sorry Ian Botham, only cricketer I can think of right now.

So, July came and with that a very hot atmosphere, I was so glad I was working in Sainsburys in the cool fridge area that was lovely but leaving work was like walking off a plane when you land in a hot country memories of a tad going to Greece which we went when I was a young lad. So, the year was going good, July the 19th Arrived my mum was on the phone to my Auntie, so wasn't really my auntie, but we called them that she I say mum's cousin but out of respect of your elders you always called your elders aunt and uncle it was called respect. That's what I was always taught by my parents. Auntie was married to Uncle, he was like a 2nd dad to me really because we as kid my sister and I and the family always liked to visit them once a year, they lived in Derbyshire and their family. Auntie who wasn't my auntie you get the drift, used to come down to our house in Surrey once a year also for the long Friday to sometime Monday, long weekend breaks bank holidays etc. So, this day of July 19th my mum was on the phone to Auntie Jennifer and she suddenly stopped, and Auntie said Are you ok Roy? He was coughing and then she said I have to go Anne that's my mum of course he is coughing up blood, my mother phones later that day to see if all was ok. Auntie said 'Yeah all good we went to the hospital she said he was checked over etc. it was a one off they said. They told them to make an appointment at the doctors of which they did, he went home had his dinner all was good, Fish & Chips. Then they left that afternoon to go and see the doctor, on the way driving down the road and suddenly whilst driving he coughed up blood again and sadly he hit a wall, he was like 2 minutes from the doctors, these people ran out, to see if all was ok and I think even the doctor who Uncle Roy knew for years came out also and they tried to help him, but very sadly he was dead. My mum called up later to see how his doctor's appointment went to be told the tragic news, when then I was absolutely numb and devastated, to say the least.

I was distraught well that was an understatement, I was so close to him we went everywhere as kids, castles, lakes Buxton, Bakewell Derbyshire, you name a place and I bet your bottom dollar we had been there. His 2 daughters my second cousins we spent days. So, as you can understand everyone was devastated the people who knew this man, he was the nicest man anyone could wish to meet! I can tell you that. So, the 19th Of July was not good, for me, or anyone involved in my family, my parents are still devastated, and the wounds will take an eternity to heal. So my health I am afraid deteriorated fast, I couldn't sleep and every time I shut my eyes I could see him and the memory of the old times we spent together came flooding back and I couldn't sleep, so I was forced to take sleeping pills every night, which I always had in reserve for odd occasions that I needed to use them! I was crying all the time, things were not good for me at this horrid time and everyone else could imagine. So, onto the funeral it was set for the 20th August in the mean time we were away on the 4th august in Selsey, wasn't really with it but was trying to be strong for the family and for the girls. I decided not to take my sleeping pills with me to Selsey and relied on drinking every night to knock me out. We went with Alana and Mick again Michilas sister and her boyfriend, we really got on rather well. Mick and I were drinking as we generally did quiet heavily as we generally did when we met up. The problem is I was waking up like 5am in the morning after not going to bed till like 1am and that's just not me, I would normally be lying in bed till like 9 or 10. So, the drink was not even knocking me out, but a mini sleeping pill could knock a 20 stone gut out, it amazes me how! So, I was having a tough time of it to say the least I was getting high, the bipolar was rearing its ugly head once again, I was now thinking the ten-year thing was becoming true! God, I hate coincidences.

So I was gambling like mad and us sufferers of bipolar know spending money is one of the evil signs that this was coming out one more, one weekend I won £400 on football betting and horse racing, I started to do like £40 to £50 at a time on a horse, I was winning and then breaking even, I was spending money like water, not good. I thought I could deal with this on my own, but no, previously we had been to a fancy dress party a week or so before we went away and I had gone as teen wolf in a basketball outfit, with lots of hair everywhere, oh obviously, the world for a lovely lady from our school Tracey 40th, she and my wife used to make an effort the wife went a Pamela Anderson from Baywatch it was a good laugh, I wasn't great at this party, I put on a happy go lucky face and people just don't know what's going on inside your head that in mental health to a t, you cannot judge a book by its cover in other words, what's inside is so much more important that the outside. I had injured my arm at work from heavy lifting and wrecked my tendons in my shoulder and was off work for 5 weeks on and off, I went back to soon thinking that I was ok, but no I had gone back and my shoulder had not repaired properly, so with that I was on co-codamol and was getting addicted to these also because it was taking the edge off my feelings and making me feel happier because I was not having a great time of it, I returned a back to work form, holiday we went on for a 5day break which was lovely for the family, but not for me

I am afraid, so got back from holiday and I decided to go and see the GP doctor and he advised me to take another 2 weeks off work which I did.

These two weeks off I was feeling very manic and high and decided to write this book, it helped me so much because it was really good therapy and helped enormously writing and getting things off my chest really, really helped me. It cleared my head and I became feeling a bit better, I was put on another drug called quetiapine 100mg a day, which I can say almost knocked my socks off to say the least, I was so drugged up, when I took these about an hour before bed, they took me into another world really, I felt so drained and found it really hard to cope, with all what was going on and I felt like another admission into that big house (hospital) was around the corner. I went to casualty because I couldn't see any specialist drs like the psychiatrist, because you have to wait quiet a long time to see these people who are specialist in their fields. So was waiting at casualty very very anxious I was to say the least, pacing up and down my wife Michila was by my side at all times, my rock, please you tube 'Come Undone' by Mr Robbie Williams and have a listen because that's what had happened to me, the words in this song was how I was feeling in this episode of my life, which was hard. I was falling to pieces, we waited 4 to 5 hours after being told by the GP that we would be fast trying to see a specialist real fast and when your high and feeling bad this is the last thing you wanted to do is sit and wait, sitting wasn't an option for me at this time. I was having a go at all the reception staff, saying I am going I have had enough of this shit, the wife was saying 'Please Darren, just wait, you have waited this long' But as much as people try to talk to you, you just don't wanna listen and believe me I just didn't want to listen. After all the waiting I got to see this guy who was there on-site psychiatrist, I went into this room and no it wasn't a blue room as before when I was younger. This time we had a try with a different team this time. So, we had a chat with this man he was asking these normal questions, are you feeling suicidal? Are you eating? Are you feeling anxious? How is your concentration? Are you feeling like you are indestructible? Which I was. But I am lucky I never really get suicidal which is good I just get angry and loose it, which is horrible for the wife to live with, I know this, this woman needs a big gold medal the size of England to put up with me. But it's not all the time, these rages just flare up, like a firework, then fizzles out, but then I am constantly doing this battle in my head, fighting with myself, which is not a pleasant experience.

So, after all this I got given, after all the questions I have answered for what it feels like a million times I got given one diazepam, which was such a waste of time. As much as they are a lovely drug, and chill you out, it soon wears off and you are back to the horrible square one so then I was passed onto the mental health team, because of my casualty visit, this is how the system in our country works. I think had a phone call the following day from a man I previously seen, which unfortunately I jumped down the poor man's throat. He offered me an appointment in a weeks' time, which I said, was not good enough how long do you have to wait I said I might be swinging from a tree before I see you. What is wrong with the system this bloody country I said he said Sorry do you want his appointment, I said to this guy don't bother I was so frustrated in how long I had to wait after feeling like this. I wasn't angry at him I was angry about the way these matters are handled.

Such delicate situations and I wonder to myself why there are so many horrible suicides in the country. But we have got to stick to the rule, so I slammed the phone down well turned the mobile off not like we use the same old-fashioned phones down, when I was young. Google 80's phones if you are not sure. Ha-ha.

So, an hour later or so when I had calmed down, I phoned him back and said I was sorry could I take this appointment after all. So, I did now I have this whole week to wait which seemed like a lifetime, longest week of my life, I can tell you.

So, I was at home this time before I was prescribed my quetiapine! So I sat at home, bearing in mind the kids were on school holidays so it made it difficult also to relax and recuperate, my parents were great they had the kids for me, which was a great help, thanks Mum and dad they were my saviours and came to the rescue a lot in my life which I am eternally grateful. My wife only worked Wed – Fri so she was around a lot also. So, his day finally came when I saw this man, I have to say was the best person I have ever seen, in his field of work. Must be so hard listening to everyone's problems all day long, but hey I know it's his job, I have to deal with quite awkward, customers at my job also, retail can be tiresome also. So, we sat down me, my wife and Dr. He was so patient with this very awkward patient: ME: but I answered his questions hey guess what, all the same questions I was asked only a week previously by the Dr at Kingston Hospital. So, I was high I was spending money like insanely, I had bought a new car £32,000.00 to be exact, during my time off work. Hey I love my car it did make me feel better and I promised my wife no more gambling if we purchased this beast of a car, I went for a lovely BMW M4 sport grand coupe, 4 wheel drive, 4 series, 3 litre god it was such a beautiful piece of machinery, it had all the gadgets I was happy, my god it cheered me up to no end. I was getting better very very slowly the drugs were working, its like the old tune, the drugs don't work they just me worse, but I know I will see your face again, thank you the verve for that song, google it if you want, no pressure though. All you young ones if your reading this book.

So still off work fortunately my bosses and Sainsburys, my store manager were so great and my line manager was absolutely so good about everything it was brilliant, couldn't ask for a better manager to understand all what I was going through, my wife had gone in my work to see him and explain everything which was happening to me and everything I had been through, I couldn't face entering my place of work because I didn't fill up to it. I had the kids in the car and was sitting in my car feeling rather subdued and he came out with a coffee in his hand, sorry I interrupted your break mate. But I was so happy to see him, it gave me a boost that day for sure. To see someone who was on my side, I know everyone else was too, but it just gave me that injection of happiness that I needed at the moment in time. He said please take all the time you need your health Is more important than the job he added, previously to me being off on holiday, I had got colleague off the week, for my hard work in helping drive the waste, but just down In our store, I was a little higher than normal in my time at work. I was doing the job as code checker because I was on light duties due to my shoulder being shot to pieces.

So I could not carry out the tasks I want to at work, which was really frustrating for my cause, I knew what I could do and what I had to achieve, because I do give 100% to my job because you can't do too much for good bosses, trouble is I do care too much about my job that is half my problem, I probably am too much which is probably not a bad thing.

During this time I was having off it didn't go to waste. I am writing this book to help other people in similar circumstances to myself and I did a bucket collection for my little girls' school, for which we collected a little over £500.00, well I did get a little more money than I would have got dressed in my own clothes. So, I decided it would be fun too stupid to dress as a woman in a blonde wig and dodgy stripy tights, I looked like Mr Tumble, well Mrs Tumble, that's what all the kids that came in the store were call me anyway, thanks Sainsburys for letting me raise money for my daughters school. It helps them get a better education I feel that I have achieved something in my life, I love doing nice things for people and societies it makes me feel good and give me a boost that I need sometimes to get me through life.

I was due back to work anyway, few days after the bucket collections we did, we like a lot of other people from the school had raised over £1200.00 for the school, which we know will be put to dam good use, a lovely school and lovely people there also.

So, I went back to work on the Sunday, Sunday's are in my shift a pattern in my job, which I don't mind because I get Saturdays off to watch my beloved AFC Wimbledon, which I enjoy it helps me relax, watching the real dons, well sometime only when we play well and win mind. I can switch off completely when I watch them and go into my own little world for going, its good therapy for me also to have an interest like this.

My daughters take it in turns to go with me, they are starting to enjoy it also and are becoming young dons. My little lucky charms, I call them.

So back to work as a code checker this job is checking dates on pretty much all the chilled dept. with a little help from my colleagues, currently our little fresh platoon. We stated to really get out teeth into driving, the waste budget down in our store. We achieved as a team getting the waste down by half which really got noticed by the management at work. The regional manager visited the store one Sunday and my store manager who was quite new to our region, probably maybe months in the job a very approachable man who had time for his work force and chatted to you like you was not just a number, very friendly indeed its got to be said. So my store manager was singing my praises to him saying I was very committed to my job asking every day to my line manager 'How is waste today?' keeping tabs on the waste budget, which I did like keeping my finger on the pulse as it were. So, my regional manager said thank you so much Darren for what you have achieved you are so important to our business. He was so thankful I really felt wanted and part of a great team! So, he said I would like to give you £20 as part of a bonus for your hard work which was so nice of him, he didn't have to thank me much appreciated, thank you.

So, I am back now in full swing of everything, achieving the highest standards which I always set myself, goal like this, think it good to do this I am feeling a lot better now. I am getting there slowly but surely, said the tortoise, that beat the hare.

My nephew who now works at the same store and dept as me I do hope he follows in my footsteps and carries on my legacy at this company, who I have given over a century of my life, well 13 years on and off, not complete service because did leave and come back. Thinking the grass was greener on the other side, but finding out it wasn't, thanks Sainsburys for believing in me again and my old manager for taking me back at work and giving me that chance, to prove myself, back in the mid 90's.

I would also like to thank my work wife, she works at our store which I have known for many years probably 24 years I would say, she always listens to my problems and my life and always is a great ear for me because a problem shared it a problem halved. Never ever bottle up your problems please talk about them when you have a mental condition because believe it helps, thanks to everyone who has listened to me in the past and the future, I can also add I am on the road to recovery now, thank you to all the NHS staff who have helped me through my up and downs and my roller coaster because life is a roller coaster and you just gotta ride it, thanks Ronan Keating, the Irish chap you made that fantastic song, it will take that as a little song quote.

So now the end is near, and I face the final curtain, well the end of this book. Remember you have to talk, don't ever bottle nothing up and you can get through this bipolar, trust me I am living proof.

You can cope and you will cope so now I will say thank you very much for buying this book online or paperback edition, I have decided to give 5% of all the royalties I get from the sales of this book to help the children of the future, because the children are out future teach them, let them lead the way, thanks Whitney, RIP. What a woman, such powerful words. So I wish to give the money to the school of which my children attend to help educate them better and bring them up to understand that trials and tribulations of life and I hope one day when there old enough they can really understand accounts of my life and hope they don't go through what I have and have the best start in life, which I had, but my path was paved by this condition what wasn't my fault and is just one of these things. So once again thank you for purchasing t it will help others for sure, so one more quote to finish I promise.

Yeah you guessed it it's gonna be a Robbie Williams, sorry the person who saved me through his power of music. That song is gonna be 'I love my life' please listen to this while you close the book, it cleared me up and will do the same for you I am sure of that, you tube it now please.

And once again 'I hope you really know me now'
Thank you
Mr D R Fry

I am cured for now, normal but what is normal and how it stays that way.

Love you all
Thanks

I wish to dedicate this book to the memory of work colleagues, friends who didn't make it through this awful ordeal of bipolar conditions

RIP my friends.